LEW BURKE'S
DOG TRAINING

by lew burke

Photography:

Frontispiece: Richard Ringoletti.

Black and white photos not specifically credited otherwise are by Manolo Guevara (pages 27, 28, 34, 48, 51, 59, 66, 71, 79, 90, 92, 111, 119, 123, 127) and Bert Torcia (pages 25, 26, 31, 36, 39, 40, 42, 49, 61, 80, 81, 89, 95, 181, 185, 186, 189, 190, 191, 196, 197, 199, 202, 206, 208, 211, 212, 215, 221, 227, 229, 235, 237, 239).

All color photos by Manolo Guevara.

ISBN 0-87666-656-X

14.⁹⁵

82 B179

Distributed in the U.S.A. by T.F.H. Publications, Inc., 211 West Sylvania Avenue, P.O. Box 27, Neptune City, N.J. 07753; in England by T.F.H. (Gt. Britain) Ltd., 13 Nutley Lane, Reigate, Surrey; in Canada to the book store and library trade by Clarke, Irwin & Company, Clarwin House, 791 St. Clair Avenue West, Toronto 10, Ontario; in Canada to the pet trade by Rolf C. Hagen Ltd., 3225 Sartelon Street, Montreal 382, Quebec; in Southeast Asia by Y.W. Ong, 9 Lorong 36 Geylang, Singapore 14; in Australia and the south Pacific by Pet Imports Pty. Ltd., P.O. Box 149, Brookvale 2100, N.S.W., Australia. Published by T.F.H. Publications Inc. Ltd., The British Crown Colony of Hong Kong.

Contents

PERSONAL ACKNOWLEDGMENTS:

To my wife, who has put up with me all these years and who has been assistant trainer, telephone service, nurse to the dogs and mother to my four children—Lizzy, Stacey, Robert and Steven.

Also, I thank Bob McAllister for his genuine friendship. He is a lover of dogs, lover of children and lover of all that is honest. He has helped me in many ways.

In addition, I would like to thank all of the entertainment world personalities who have helped me to find the opportunity to show my work. Special thanks in this regard go to Soupy Sales, and I would like also to thank Johnny Carson, Merv Griffin, Mike Douglas, David Frost, Jerry Lewis, Captain Kangaroo, and all the others such as Goodson & Toddman for having allowed me to perform on their shows.

Most of all, I thank my parents, who have been praying for safety and happiness for their sometimes impulsive son. I now know how difficult their job was.

PREFACE

This book is bound to stimulate much controversy in the circles of dog trainers, veterinarians, animal behaviorists and psychologists.

The use of the pack leadership theory as the main motivating factor in the relationship between dog and man is expounded clearly and succinctly. Animal behaviorists and psychologists, like their counterparts in the human field, have many different theories and methods of utilizing and implementing these theories to modify and elicit desired behavior patterns and responses. Lew has applied the pack leadership theory to achieve ultimate results in the field of dog training.

The most important contribution of this book is that the methods outlined in it work. All theories of behavior rise and fall in popularity; eventually the pack theory may be disproved, but the methods developed by Lew Burke will always be valid. Other methods of dog training may, in many cases, be successful, but fall short with difficult and problem dogs. If it is possible to train a dog—and we must realize that some dogs cannot be trained—Lew's methods will work.

Lew Burke has trained my own dog and many other dogs for my clients, and the results have been astounding. As a veterinarian I deal with dogs every day, and I pride myself in being able to relate, control and handle almost any dog I've seen. My own personal dog, however, was a source of frustration to me. As hard as I tried I couldn't get through to him and finally contacted Lew. Lew trained both my dog and myself [this is a very important part of Lew's program] and the result has been another happy dog and owner.

The combination of love, security and reward balanced by authority and discipline [administered correctly] produces the ultimately desired behavior patterns and responses in the most efficient and painless manner possible.

The key to Lew's method is in sensitivity to the animal's wants and needs coupled with a sense of timing of when and how to reinforce a dog's behavior. To be sensitive to a dog's needs requires knowledge of the dog on three levels. The levels are genetic background, environmental background and the dog's human or social background. The timing is something that must be carefully developed and must be extremely flexible depending on the individual dog and the dog's own mood at the time. I cannot recommend this book highly enough to any dog owner, trainer, veterinarian or anyone else who seeks to understand dogs and their relation to man.

S.J. Schimelman, D.V.M.
Somers Animal Hospital
Somers, N.Y. 10589

LEW BURKE'S
DOG TRAINING

The author and Buddy, his highly trained German Shepherd. A show business personality in his own right, Lew Burke still makes appearances on television but is more actively engaged in the operation of his dog training center in Carmel, New York.

WHY PAY ATTENTION TO THIS BOOK?

Any reader of this book has a right to be. . . in fact, *should* be. . . concerned with determining just what gives me the right to set myself up as an authority on the subject of training dogs. I certainly hope that what I say and show in this book, coupled with your own successful experiences in applying my methods, will prove to you that I know what I'm talking about. But just in case you're wondering about my qualifications and would like to be reassured that my advice is based on solid experience and backed up by demonstrable success in the field of dog training *before* you start to put my recom-

Soupy Sales plays with Buddy while Lew Burke offers encouragement and Mike Douglas looks on in this scene from the *Mike Douglas Show.*

mendations into practice, consider that I have been or currently am:

Trainer for 20th Century Fox films.

Trainer for Columbia films.

I have worked with Warner Bros. and other major film studios. . . and here are some of the motion pictures with which I and dogs trained by me have been connected: *The Hot Rock*, with George Segal and Robert Redford. . . *The Exorcist* . . . *For Pete's Sake*, with Barbara Streisand. . . *The Happy Hooker*, with Lynn Redgrave. . . *The Marathon Man,* starring Sir Laurence Olivier and Dustin Hoffman.

Trainer of Buddy, a dog featured with me on national television shows more than 40 times at press date. Here are just some of the television shows and television personalities with whom Buddy and I have worked: *Tonight Show* with Johnny Carson. . . Merv Griffin. . . Mike Douglas. . . David Frost. . . *Wonderama*. . . Muscular Dystrophy Telethon with Jerry Lewis. . . *Captain Kangaroo*. . . *What's My Line*. . . *To Tell The Truth*. . . *Bozo The Clown*, and others.

Trainer of dogs employed to protect industrial plants.

And how about this, from Bob McAllister of *Wonderama:*

As the host of what many people consider the most prestigious children's show on commercial television, I have the tremendous responsibility of presenting what I consider to be the most entertaining and enlightening subjects to children.

A number of years ago, my staff informed me that they had booked an act on a future Wonderama *show that they thought would be great. The act was Lew Burke and his dog, Buddy. Normally I have*

Lew Burke retires to a neutral corner after scoring a knockdown in his second Golden Gloves boxing match; this was his second first-round knockout.

complete confidence in my staff's judgment, but a question arose in my mind.

I have hosted children's shows for twenty years and have become wary of animal acts. My reasons, I think, are well justified, since I've been exposed to unbelievable acts of cruelty to animals — performers using shock devices, beating animals unmercifully and just using the animals as a way to gain notoriety for themselves. My staff informed me that in this case my negative thinking was unjustified.

The day of the taping came and my schedule

Lynn Redgrave and Buddy relax together on the set of the motion picture *The Happy Hooker*.

was such that I didn't have time to get acquainted with this act until minutes before taping. I found out, much to my amazement, that Lew Burke, looking a little like Steve Lawrence, was a Golden Gloves boxer at one time, a school teacher with a Masters Degree, a comic who played the "Borscht Belt" for several years but, even more important, a real lover of dogs.

The director spoke over the intercom, "Tape is rolling." The floor manager cued me and I said, "Youngsters, for the first time on Wonderama *it gives me a great deal of pleasure to introduce Lew Burke and Buddy."*

Lew walked on stage with one of the most beautiful German Shepherds I've ever seen. The dog was wagging his tail the entire time. Lew said, pointing to his faithful companion, "For the purpose of identification, this is Buddy." The children were delighted.

From that point on Buddy performed absolute miracles under the direction of Lew, who showed true affection for his pet.

Since that first appearance on Wonderama, *Lew and Buddy have appeared more than any other variety act on our show.*

Lew and his family have become the closest of friends with me and my family. He has personally trained my dog. And as far as I'm concerned Lew has more knowledge than anyone else about the behavior of animals.

Love is the keynote—never have I met a man with more understanding than Lew Burke, a dog's best friend!

And here are some of the things said about me and Buddy by people in a position to know:

Earl Wilson — *"Buddy is the smartest dog alive."*

Barbra Streisand — (After completion of film *"For*

Pete's Sake.) "*For Lew Burke—Thanks a lot, Lew—Buddy was terrific.*"

Johnny Carson — "*Very good!*" (about the act)

Merv Griffin — "*Very good — marvelous.*"

Gary Moore — "*Magnificent. The most magnificently disciplined animal I have ever met.*"

Bennet Cerf — "*Buddy is smarter than some authors I know.*"

Gil Fates (producer) — "*Thanks for your fine job on* What's My Line. *Hope you enjoyed it as much as our audience.*"

Soupy Sales — "*To Lew—the greatest dog trainer in the whole world.*"

Mike Douglas — "*Too much! Great act!*"

David Frost — "*Remarkable, just brilliant.*"

Father Keith Mahoney (Mt. Carmel Carmelite Fathers, Williamstown, Mass.) — "*Every dog I have ever brought to you, from German Shepherd to Bichon Frise, has turned out beautifully. What I especially admire is your ability to train a dog without injuring its temperament. Every dog you have done for me has responded completely, but also happily. This must be as much art as it is skill.*"

How the Dog Sees Himself Within the Family

Before starting to teach any dog, the teacher should be familiar with how a dog thinks.

In its natural habitat, the wild, the dog belongs to a pack. If he is not the pack leader, he fits somewhere within the hierarchy of the pack. If he does not obey the laws of the pack, the leader will make certain that he complies. If the leader is not successful, a new pack leader will be born.

When we take a dog into our home, as far as he is concerned he belongs to a pack. No dog ever turns on his master. Instead, he challenges for leadership. Therefore, if you are to be the pack leader, you must have a way of maintaining control as far as the dog is concerned. You must be able to establish definite rules and regulations which the dog as a pack member can never deviate from. If you are successful in enforcing your rules 99% of the time, you are not the genuine pack leader. The 99% control will slip to 95% and then to 90%—eventually, if the dog has a drive toward achieving pack leadership, he might eventually challenge. Fortunately for most people, most dogs would prefer to remain as pack members. "Buddy" is a pack leader.

We do not gain 100% control or despotic power over the dog as the pack leader does in the wild if we employ such methods as hitting, kicking or in some other way abusing the animal. The dog will only come to mistrust those who strike him and will eventually bite out of fear and in order to protect himself.

The animal doesn't just pick up on your rules and man-made mores. This anthropomorphic instinct is never present. Anthropomorphic views inspired through fairy tales, fables and motion pictures will lead only to frustration for the dog and the family.

You must teach a person from infancy to adulthood. The same is true with the dog, but success with the dog can be achieved in a much shorter period of time. One thing is certain: you must first decide what your rules are and then communicate them to your dog. Once he understands, he will be a much happier pack member, simply because all dogs are by their nature dependent. The dog wants a leader. He wants someone to lean on. He wants approval from his pack leader. It is your responsibility to educate your dog for his own welfare and happiness. If you don't, you shouldn't own him.

Once the dog understands clearly what you want from him, what his responsibilities are, he will respond in the hope of gaining your approval. This does not mean that your three-year-old or eight-year-old child will have the same control as you. As far as the dog is concerned, he has one pack leader. The others in the family are pack members, each possessing a definite position within the family hierarchy. He may adore the three-year-old but certainly won't obey him as he would the pack leader. The three-year-old is not physically or mentally capable of controlling the dog. The dog will obey each family member in direct proportion to that member's standing in the pack. One adult may get 90% control, whereas another will get 95%. The amount of control you obtain will depend upon your own ability to apply what this book will try to teach you: namely, how to achieve pack leadership.

You should never ask a dog to do something unless you want it—but after you ask for it, you'd better make certain you get it. Having your orders obeyed is a *basic* requirement in maintaining leadership. Naturally, while teaching a new concept, you can't get what you ask for; however, once learning has been completed, then enforcement is mandatory. This doesn't mean that you have to be cruel. On the contrary, you must be strong and yet offer love at the same time. The better you are able to combine these ingredients, the better pack leader you will become.

Normal dogs will not bite newborn infants. Because of its body chemistry, an infant resembles a new-born puppy whom the dog adopts as his own. You will often see the three-year-old getting away with ear- and tail-pulling that the more mature youngster will not get away with. This distinction is the result of chemistry. The older children are older pack members; the dog will defend them and play with them as a pack member but will not tolerate the same abuse from them as he would from a younger pack member. If the youngster offers ear-pulling, eye-gouging or tail-pulling to the dog, naturally the dog will eventually come to mistrust the family pack member. Therefore, the family pack members and pack leader should be educated on how to treat the dog just as the dog must be taught how to live within the pack.

The dog should never be left unsupervised with a pack member who is not capable of physical control. The dog might play with this pack member as he would with another dog—and this play can be rough and might result in physical harm unknown to the dog. If the dog is to be left free, there should always be some pack member present who is capable of assuming pack leadership. Some very young children are capable of assuming this role with very many dogs; with other dogs, not even the man in the house is capable. Dogs and people are all individuals. Some people are stronger-willed than others, and some dogs have stronger drives to be pack leaders.

The dog who is aggressive can be taught not to be. Regardless of his problem or misbehavior, it can be corrected. I have never met a dog who could not be taught obedience. But only through proper education can the dog be made to clearly understand his proper place within your pack. The job of educating him—making him understand his place—is up to you.

My aim in this book is to relay knowledge so that dog owners can correctly train their own dogs for obedience, advanced obedience, housebreaking and protection work while allowing them the fun and luxury of trick work at no extra cost. My dog Buddy has appeared on television with Johnny Carson, Merv Griffin, Mike Douglas, David Frost and Jerry Lewis, and on *Wonderama, What's My Line, To Tell the Truth* and a variety of other shows. He has astonished the public when he responded to math questions by walking around a circle of numbers and picking up the correct answer. (The reader will be taught how to teach his dog this trick as well as the other tricks Buddy can do.)

My Personal Introduction to the Work

A dog can only be as good as the person who handles him, and it is impossible for an uninformed trainer to obtain the same results as a trainer who is armed with facts. Once you have the knowledge, your desire, persistence, self-discipline and talent will directly affect the final results. My method is based on the fact that a dog is a dog. He is not an intelligent pupil with human logic, but rather an animal who lives in a world without human logic. To the dog, black is black and white is white, so to speak. Learning is not accomplished through logical thinking, but solely through the faculty of memory presented through the medium of dog psychology... never *human* psychology. That is what I will attempt to spell out in this book.

People who make the mistake of thinking that dogs are endowed with human understanding and morals never can attain a real relationship with their dogs. My approach results in a happier, healthier dog as well as a genuine relationship. The animal will not be required to master any command exceeding his powers of comprehension. The trainer will avoid disappointment and annoyance, for he will clearly understand the dog's abilities and will, for the first time in his life, attain real communication.

I didn't become a dog trainer overnight, and neither will you. It took me many long years of close observation, experimentation and dedication to the idea of doing a job right to learn what I have learned. It's going to take some effort on your part, too; luckily, though, you'll be starting out with an entire set of pre-digested data, so your work will be a lot easier. But please bear in mind this very important point: read the whole book, not just selected portions of it that you think have the greatest degree of applicability to your particular situation, before you begin training your dog according to my methods. Just as I have developed my techniques over a period of time, I've also presented them over a number of different portions of this book; no one portion contains the whole story, so don't expect it to. Read the book to get a clearer picture of my view of dog psychology, and *then* begin your training. Also, you are going to see certain key concepts repeated many times. I have deliberately repeated myself exactly because of the importance of the concepts involved; they are important enough to bear repetition to the point of annoyance. If you're annoyed by seeing the same advice given five times in five different places, I'm sorry, but it's for your own and your dog's benefit.

Good reading, good luck.

Basic and Advanced Obedience—voice command and hand signals

We already know that dogs instinctively belong to packs. Being intrinsically dependent animals, they need someone to lean on. You, the owner, must become the leader of the pack in domesticated life. If you are not the leader you should not own the dog. You must offer love and strength simultaneously. The more efficiently and effectively you do this, the better leader you are. This is the psychological approach that is employed in teaching any command in which the dog is near you.

One should never start to work with any dog until a warm relationship has been established. If the dog is forced to comply to any command by someone he has no love for, the command will forever be an unpleasant memory. Therefore it is a good idea to feed your dog by hand for several days before training begins. Play with him. Roughhouse with him, as dogs do with each other. Allow him to sit on the couch with you, and lovingly stroke his head and body. *Never* reprimand him or scold him after calling him to you, because his limited intelligence allows him to associate the scolding only with the act he performed most recently—in this case, the act of coming to you and being near you. He must always associate being near you with love, warmth, food and pleasure. Never pain. In a later chapter I will clearly explain how to correct your dog when he does something that doesn't fit into your generally accepted scheme. If you don't want him on your couch, then find some other place the two of you can be cuddly. Once you see that your dog loves to be near you, it is time to move on to the next step.

No animal should suddenly be exposed to a new learning situation if he is not properly prepared. Therefore, we never put a collar and leash on a dog and immediately start him on "heel." He must first become accustomed to wearing the collar and leash so that they receive a pleasurable association. If he is to feel discomfort of any sort, you, the trainer, should not be associated with it. Therefore, put any loosely fitting Nylon or chain collar around his neck and allow him to run freely for several hours. Repeat this for two or three days. When he no longer pays attention to the collar, attach a six-foot web lead and allow him to run freely for several hours. Feed him by hand after you attach the lead. Continue this procedure for several days until you see he does not object.

If a dog has not previously been on the lead, it will do a great deal of harm to take him for a walk on a short lead, especially with a spiked collar, and drag him along. The dog will become fearful of you and totally distracted; teaching him anything thereafter will prove quite difficult and unpleasant for the both of you. Fear should *never* be aroused in the dog while he is on the lead. Once the dog has become accustomed to the lead, it is time to go on to the next step.

People very often have erroneous conceptions about the psychology of animals. Movies, fables and fairy tales often present to us living animals who think, understand human speech and perform

Some of the most important pieces of equipment in using Lew Burke's training methods: left to right, length of dowel, switch; *bottom of photo*, left to right, prong collar, handle, throw chain (center of photo), choke collar (lower center), stall chain with snaps attached at both ends; *top of photo*, long web lead, short web lead.

moral and immoral acts. We can save ourselves much disappointment and insure the animal's cheerful and rapid learning by allowing him to learn *his* way, the canine way. Human psychology and dog psychology are completely different; dog psychology actually should be called a parapsychology.

Let me make one point crystal clear if I haven't already done so. Dogs don't speak or understand our language. They learn because they are compelled to respond and know that they are correct only because of your positive reaction through happy and excited voice, patting the animal and/or using food as a reward. Once communication has been accomplished and the dog responds to your command, stop using food as a reward. Just give praise. Food is only sometimes used to aid in communication. If used after learning has been achieved, it becomes a fake reward that causes the dog to work for food, not for you. Your praise should be all that is necessary.

When the dog you are training trusts the lead, he will thrust his head to you while you attach the leash to the collar. It is now time to introduce him to the prong or spiked collar.

A prong collar's relatively limited constriction and wide bearing surface, together with the shortness of the stubs (prongs), creates less of a possibility of injuring the dog with this type of training col-

This stall chain has been semi-permanently attached to the screw-eye and S-hook arrangement, because the loop of the S-hook holding the chain has been crimped back; the stall chain therefore cannot be slipped out of the S-hook without use of a tool to pry open the hook.

Both the Samoyed and the Boxer have been attached by variations in the S-hook and stall chain technique. It is not cruel to circumscribe the movements of a dog during a sensible training program, and neither of these dogs is suffering.

Proper attachment of the choke collar, whether pronged or not pronged, is very important. See pages 97 and 100 for a complete sequence of photos showing step-by-step correct attachment proce-dures. (Prong collar sequence on page 97; plain choke collar on page 100.)

lar than with others with which I am familiar. An analysis by engineers would verify this. The prong collar will afford quicker and better results for the novice, and consequently the dog will require fewer corrections. Besides, the prong will afford more definite pack leadership, as corrections will be more clear to the animal. Unfortunately, the prong looks like a cruel, clumsy device. If it weren't for this, the arguments against it might not exist. However, you may use either a choker or prong collar. Either will suffice. I recommend the prong, especially for novices. Results will be attained more quickly with less stress put upon the dog. After you adjust the prong collar so that it constricts and opens easily, and so that it is comfortable to the dog, give him a piece of food and leave the collar on. The following day you will move on to the next step, which is as follows: screw an eye-screw (also called screw-eye) into the baseboard of a wall. Attach one end of an S-hook to the eye-screw and secure it with a pliers. The other end of the S-hook is secured to the end link of a chain lead. Attach the end of the chain lead to the dog's collar and leave him there for 15 to 30 minutes. At first he might pull forward but will stop when he feels the prong collar around his neck. He will quickly stop trying to get free. He will realize that whenever he pulls he feels the prongs—but he never will associate this discomfort with you. After all, you're out of the room. After a short period the dog will accept his bondage.

The reason for the stall chain is to acquaint the dog with the feeling of the prong-caused constrictions around his neck without associating them with you. Each time he pulls, he feels the pressure of the prongs. But you are not there, so how can he blame you? So when you walk him and make necessary corrections, he will not associate the tightening of his collar with you. This will afford the opportunity of not allowing the dog to think at any time that his trainer is responsible for enforcement of his actions.

During this period, place some of the dog's favorite treats in a small fishing bag (carrying case) which is to be attached to your belt. Return to the room. Your dog should immediately react happily upon seeing you. If he does not, he is not ready for you to begin training. Once he has grown to love you, then and only then do you start your work.

TEACHING TO HEEL

When the leash is held loosely, the dog must follow its master at his left side. The lead should never have to be pulled tight regardless of whether or not the handler speeds up, slows down or suddenly turns left or right or about. The chest of the dog should be almost perfectly in line with the left knee of the trainer so that the handler may keep the dog constantly in view through the employment of peripheral vision.

It is now time for you to play good guy once again. You will attach the six-foot webbed lead to the collar and release the dog from the chain. As far as he is concerned, you have just given him freedom. To increase his joy and pleasure, you are to take him out onto the street for a "fun walk." Generally, he will pull ahead of you excitedly. This is a good response. If he lags behind or shows fear of any type, encourage him by fondling his head with your left hand, which is free from the lead. Or bend forward at the waist and clap your hands excitedly. This will inspire his chase instinct. As he comes to the desired position, praise him lavishly and give

The correct starting position for teaching the dog to heel.

(Additional step-by-step photos showing the sequence of training to heel can be seen on pages 101 and 104.)

Correcting the dog that has turned too far to the right while being trained to heel: snap the lead leftward and move the right knee into him. If your dog doesn't respond satisfactorily after several days, don't be afraid to snap the lead with more authority. The discomfort the dog receives must be strong enough to make the point clear. Two or three sharp corrections are preferable to many overly mild (and therefore useless) corrections.

31

him some food—one or two pieces. If he pulls ahead, you should gently snap (not pull) the leash backward and simultaneously tap your left side. When he gets to the desired position, praise him lavishly and offer food. The leash should never be held taut, for then it will not be relaxed, and a tug of war and panic will result. A snapping action is like that of a rubber band. You quickly snap the lead with your wrist and arm and just as quickly relax, allowing the desired amount of slack to return. If the snapping is done sharply and quickly, the dog will soon realize that it is far more pleasurable to be next to his master's side than to be away. But remember. . . snap the lead with love.

If the dog continues to forge ahead, quickly turn about so that you are now going in the opposite direction. As you turn about, immediately snap the leash and simultaneously tap your left side with your left palm. This correction employs opposite momentum and is the very best. As the dog comes to your left side, praise him lavishly and excitedly and offer food. He will not associate you with the collar pinching his neck, but rather will associate the pleasure of your praise and food reward with both the word "heel" (which you will have uttered coincidental with snapping the lead and tapping your side) and the tapping at your side. Upon arriving at the correct position, he will have the sense of having done right. If he should step too far to the left, snap the lead to the right; if he should step too far to the right, snap the lead to the left and turn into him so that your right knee bumps his chin. Always simultaneously happily and excitedly say "Heel" and tap your left side. Immediately offer verbal praise and food reward when he reaches the proper position. He will quickly realize that the word "heel" or just the simple tapping of your left side will result in pleasure when he gets to your knee. And if he is not quick enough in getting there, he will somehow feel the discomfort of the prongs around his neck. He prefers to be at your left side than away from it simply because you are the leader of the pack. He has always received food and pleasurable caressing when he is near you, and now whenever he hears the word "heel" or the tapping of the side he receives discomfort which is quickly replaced by pleasure once he gets close to you again. Just as not every trainer possesses the same skills, not every dog learns at the same speed. Don't ever get angry, and never shout. Give each command in a soft but positive voice. Your anger or nervousness will upset the dog and may cause him to panic. If this happens, stop the lesson for a brief moment to reassure your pal, and then continue to work. Before going on stage with Buddy, I keep away from him if I am nervous, because I don't want to transmit my nervousness to him. His performance is always better when my spirits are up.

The appropriate management of the leash is as follows: the left hand grasps the lead in such a way that the dog is brought into the desired position, with his chest almost exactly in line with the trainer's left knee.

The right hand also holds the lead. In this way, if the animal bounds forward he can be snapped back with the right hand while the lead is allowed to slip through the left hand. If a chain lead is used, the trainer will receive burns on his palm. If you grasp the lead with your right hand, the left hand is left free and can be used to attract the dog to one's side by caressing gestures. The trainer should always walk and work his dog in new territories so that new

Lavish praise should be the dog's reward for having performed correctly when being taught to heel and many other lessons. The affectionate pat and recognizably loving and encouraging tone of his true pack leader are truly satisfying rewards for any dog.

distractions are constantly encountered. Whenever the dog's attention wanders, even slightly, he should immediately be snapped.

Be certain not to exceed 25 minutes for each session on "heel." If you do, the exercise will become tedious and boring. Always end each session with the dog responding correctly three or four times in succession. He must finish each training session being correct and positive and receiving praise and food. At the end of each session say "**Okay**" and give the dog more food, but do not take off the lead just yet. We don't want him to think that when the lead comes off it signifies freedom; we want "okay" to mean freedom. Don't take off the lead until he's been free for several minutes. Depending upon the abilities of the trainer and dog, generally after five to ten sessions your dog should clearly understand and perform "heel" and love to be at that position at your side. At this point we start to teach the automatic "sit."

TEACHING TO SIT

The trainer must know that the severity of correction and strength he employs when snapping the lead must be governed by the aptitude shown by the individual dog. He should always employ encouragement with every dog, especially with those that are timid. The more praise you offer, the better the chances that you will not ruin your dog's aptitude. You can never offer too much love after your dog responds correctly. When the handler or trainer stops walking, the dog must sit automatically and without hesitation.

If you were walking with your dog and met someone you wanted to speak with, it would be impossible to do so unless your dog stopped moving. Therefore, he should sit instantly and not move until you have finished your conversation and have decided to walk; at this point you would tell your dog to "heel" and you would go off together.

The mechanics of teaching the dog to sit go this way: one hand grasps the dog under the chest and the other is placed on top of his hindquarters. By means of appropriate pressure with both hands the dog is made to assume the sitting position. This must be coordinated with your giving the word "Sit." When he sits, immediately praise him, offering a food reward. Repeat this several times until the dog's resistance to your pressure becomes slight. As soon as the dog has become accustomed to being made to sit in this way, take hold of the lead and very gently snap up while the other hand presses down the hindquarters to the sound of the command "Sit." Again offer verbal and food reward. Repeat several times until the dog seems to be sitting only with the tugging upward of the lead.

Using the hip to induce the dog to take up the sitting position.

Now grasp the lead with your right hand. Give the command "**Heel**," take a step and then stop. After a brief second, say "**Sit**"; simultaneously lean your left hip as close to the dog's side as you can, and at the very same moment snap the lead up. When he responds correctly, offer food and verbal praise. The movement of your hip into him will induce him to want to sit, and the compulsion will come from the upward snap of the lead. Stand next to your dog for a few minutes. Each time he moves even slightly, instantly repeat the command "**Sit**" and simultaneously gently snap the lead up. Repeat this exercise for fifteen to twenty minutes. After two or three days the dog should sit automatically whenever you stop walking. If he does not respond immediately, increase the sharpness of the snapping of the lead, but never increase the violence of your voice. The offering of verbal and food praise remains constant. Once the dog starts to sit instantly, stop using the food. The only reward he is to be offered for automatically sitting is your praise. Food is used only to assist in making communication. Once the command "sit" is thoroughly understood and performed you can increase the velocity of response by using a switch—a thin green branch from a tree. Hold the switch in your right hand, hiding it from the dog's view with your body. Keep your right arm extended at your side. Hold the lead in your left hand. Take two or three steps; the moment you stop walking say "**Sit**," and at that exact moment gently flick the switch behind you, using only your wrist, and make certain it hits the top of the dog's hindquarters. The flick of the wrist can be light—no pain is necessary. As you do this, snap the lead up with your left hand. All this must be perfectly coordinated. If you are not able to, don't try. Repeat this until the reaction is to your complete satisfaction. Never telegraph the use of the switch. The dog should not ever see it strike him, for anticipation of it can cause him to panic.

If your dog should decide to lie down instead of sitting, say "Sit" and snap up on your lead; with the switch tap lightly at the dog's toes. If he doesn't sit, tap harder and snap the lead with more sharpness. With this correction, the dog may see the switch. There is no danger of negative results. He will quickly overcome this problem.

TEACHING TO HEEL OFF THE LEAD

Once the dog responds to the heel and the automatic sit perfectly on the lead, take off the lead. In an enclosed area say "Heel." The moment the dog's attention wanders, gently toss the throw chain at his side; at the same instant repeat the verbal command "Heel," tap your left side and continue walking and moving away from your pet. His pack instinct will arouse his need to get close to your side where he feels the safety and comfort of being next to his pack leader rather than being away and feeling the discomfort or sudden fear of the chain against his side. After several repetitions, he will stick close to your side where he feels safe rather than wander away where he is discomfited by the chain. After several repetitions, if his attention wanders or distractions cause him to lose attention, you will merely have to rattle the chain and he will return to your side.

TEACHING THE SIT—STAY

The dog's natural instinct is to follow you, his pack leader. Therefore, you must compel him to stay.

With the dog at the heel and automatic sit position, say "Stay" and at the very same moment place your open left palm in front of his nose. Holding the lead in your right hand, take one step forward and turn left so that you face your dog squarely. As you do so, hold the lead straight up, disallowing any slack, repeat "Stay" and keep your open left palm in front of his face. Continue to say "Stay," keeping

The beginning position in teaching the sit-stay command. (See page 108 for other photos showing the sit-stay sequence of training.)

Jerking up the lead and positioning the palm in front of the dog's face during teaching of the sit-stay command. (Other photos showing techniques involved in teaching the sit-stay command appear on page 108.)

your open palm in front of his face and the lead held straight up. Then return to him and offer food and praise. The open palm in front of his face and the lead extended tight and over his head will compel him to stay. He will be reassured by your praise and food reward. Continue this procedure until you can walk out to the full extent of the six-foot lead. You will feel when your dog doesn't try to follow you or move toward you. At this time, allow your left arm to drop so that the lead now has slack in it. Continue to repeat the command "Stay," now keeping your right arm extended and parallel to the ground, with your open palm in the direction of the dog's face. If he should start towards you, quickly snap up on the lead so that the bottom of the collar jerks up against the underpart of his jaw. Take one step toward him, repeat the command "Stay" and project your open right palm at his face. He'll be compelled to stay. Immediately return to him and offer food and praise. Once he seems to grasp this while at the end of the lead, move in clockwise and counterclockwise directions, always instantly ready upon his breaking to repeat "Stay," accompanied by keeping your open palm in front of his face and snapping up the lead. If he should continue to break by trying to follow you, either toss the chain lightly at his chest as you say "Stay" or tap him with the switch on the chest. Either inducement will work.

Repeat the procedure for 20 to 30 minutes for several days. Do not try this off lead until he has 100% performance while on lead. If he breaks when off the lead, toss the throw chain or use the switch and by all means do so by going back to the employment of the lead.

TEACHING THE DOWN COMMAND

In teaching "down," the capacity of the dog to learn is reinforced by his submissive instinct.

The effect of the compulsion necessary to teach "down" is first intimidating to the dog. The effect is eliminated as soon as the dog has learned that nothing disagreeable happens to him after he has lain down and while he remains in that position. Until he becomes accustomed to dropping immediately on his own accord upon hearing the command and/or seeing the hand signal, training should take place only on the lead. Otherwise the instinct to run away comes into play. This must under all circumstances be prevented from the onset.

One begins with a mild form of compulsion. The dog is gently pressed to the ground and held there. Then say "**Down.**" Praise him and offer food. After several repetitions, stand facing the dog. Put a foot over the lead in such a way that it is between the

Praising the dog who has attained the desired position during teaching of the down command. (Other photos showing teaching of the down command are on page 109.)

heel and sole of your shoe to insure easy sliding of the lead.

With the dog in the Sit-Stay position, say "**Down**" and immediately extend your right arm straight over your head. Keep your arm extended until the dog is all the way down. This will become the visual or hand signal. Continue to repeat the command "**Down**" as you pull the lead upward from under your shoe. Your pulling up will compel the dog to move down. If he starts to panic, don't stop. Immediately drop the throw chain on the back of his neck and continue to pull up. As soon as he is down, praise lavishly and offer food. Because the action is incomprehensible to the animal, he will at first wish to get up again, but he is kept in this position by your use of your foot on the lead and your arm holding the lead up tight. Leave him in the down position for several moments and continue to reassure through praise and food.

Allow the lead to slacken. If the dog tries to get up, immediately renew counter-pressure on the lead while giving the "down" command and the hand signal. Again give praise.

The preliminary practice should only last a few minutes. After the dog responds to the command "**Down**" two or three times on his own, stop the lesson.

If after 10 or 15 repetitions the animal still resists going down to any degree, you can hasten the learning process by snapping the lead downward with your wrist or by stepping down on the taut lead.

TEACHING THE DOWN—STAY

After the animal responds to the down command immediately, leave him there for long periods of time, saying "**Stay**" while using your open palm to project the feeling and allowing the lead to remain attached to his collar. If he breaks, toss the throw chain at him immediately, repeating "**Down**." If he manages to run off, go after him and bring him back to where you originally told him to stay and force him to go down exactly where you left him. Then praise and say "**Stay**." Every so often, offer food and praise while keeping him in the down-stay posture.

After he seems to be completely under control, attach the 20-foot lead to his collar and tie the end of it to a post. Say "**Stay**" and walk away 30 or 40 feet. If the dog decides to get up, at that very moment say "**No**" and then say "**Down**," and at the same moment toss the throw chain, trying to hit the dog at his side. If he goes down, reassure him through praise and food. If he does not lie down, take hold of the lead and snap him down. Then give him praise— but only after you win.

Take off the lead only after the dog responds 100%. If mistakes occur off lead, return to the use of the lead.

Incidentally, this is the first occasion we've had to tell the dog "**No**," so in the discussion of the next command I'll talk about what "**No**" means to him.

TEACHING THE SIT FROM THE DOWN POSITION

With the dog in the down-stay position, walk in and say "**Sit**" as you gently pull up on the lead; if he is not sitting by the time your feet reach him, gently apply pressure upon his paws by pressing down on them with the soles of your feet. When he sits, praise him and offer food.

By holding the food up over his head, you will induce him to sit—the other inducements are the pulling up of the lead and the pressure on his paws. Remember—the greater control you have, the better pack leader you are and the happier your dog will be.

Dogs don't reason the way people do. To the dog, black is black and white is white, so to speak; there is no middle ground. Therefore, he is either allowed to do something or he is not allowed.

There can never be two sets of rules. He is allowed to jump on people or he is not. (He can't differentiate between a clean suit that you don't want him to jump on and working clothes that you don't care about, so to keep him from messing up the suit you have to prevent him from messing up the work clothes, too. He has no discretion and cannot be given any leeway to choose.) He is allowed to chew shoes or he is not. (He doesn't know that you like the new shoes and don't care about the old ones.)

He is allowed to jump on the couch or he is not. As far as he is concerned, the bed is as good as the couch. So you must decide firstly what rules you wish to establish—and you must not deviate once a rule is established.

Apparently when an animal performs a voluntary act, he does so to satisfy his own needs. However, if at the precise moment he is attaining pleasure he immediately experiences an unpleasant sensation stronger in intensity than the pleasurable one, and if this unpleasant sensation takes place each time he begins his pleasurable experience, the pleasurable experience will cease to be pleasurable.

For example, your dog goes onto the couch, and you don't want him there. You never call the dog to come to you and then scold him when he gets there. If you do this, he will not come to you again. While he is on the couch, say "No" and simultaneously throw the chain and hit him. He will jump off the couch. You walk over to him and praise him by saying "Good puppy." As far as the dog is concerned,

Dog owners can set their own standards for acceptable behavior from their dogs, but once they have decided to condemn a certain action they have to remain consistent in its condemnation. They can't allow the performance of a condemned action at one time and get excited about it when the dog does the same thing another time. . . the dog has no way of knowing the circumstances behind why something might be okay to do one day and forbidden the next. Sitting on furniture is an example. If you want the dog to stay off the furniture, keep him off all of the furniture, and keep him off all the time, not just those times when you're in the mood to enforce your commands. A throw chain that comes whistling through the air at the dog is an effective deterrent, and if the chain is tossed consistently each and every time the dog climbs up onto a forbidden spot, it doesn't take long for him to get the idea that climbing on furniture is going to result in having the sinister (to him) chain attack him. He doesn't like being subjected to attacks by the chain, and therefore he refrains from doing the things that in his mind are associated with a certain attack by the chain.

you are still a nice guy. He was on the couch and the chain showed up to do the dirty work. The moment he jumped off the couch, you praised him. It is much more pleasurable to be off the couch and hear praise than to be on the couch and receive the frightening sound of the chain.

If you throw the chain effectively and it hits the dog on your first several attempts, you will later only have to rattle it or merely say "**No.**" This procedure can be used to stop unnecessary barking, chewing, etc. But remember, you must catch the dog in the act of the undesirable behavior and throw the chain at that moment. Immediately follow with praise.

A stronger compulsion in enforcing the command "no" is the use of the switch. Use of the switch is not necessary, however, except in extremely negative and persistent behavioral patterns—for example, dog fighting. This problem can offer serious danger to master, friends and dog. When a dog is in a dog fight, his frenzy becomes so intensified that in the heat of battle the dog will bite anything he sees in front of him or feels on his body. He does so because he is fighting to survive and therefore is in a severe state of fright. He will chew on his master, not realizing it is his master. Therefore, this problem should be arrested as soon as it starts. Keep the dog on lead. When he demonstrates aggression of any kind toward another dog who is passing, swat him across the side of the face and on the backside, saying "**No!**" He must go into submission. Your application should be applied in direct proportion to the intensity of the overt behavioral pattern. The same method should be employed with dogs who attempt to bite people without provocation. Again, these problems can result in the death of

To break the dog of annoying habits like jumping up onto people—and this is one of the most annoying habits a dog can develop, since it is especially repugnant to people who have an active fear of dogs regardless of their size—the dog has to be subjected to an unpleasant sensation every time he performs the action. A sharp rap in the pit of the stomach with the knee can have the desired deterrent effect, especially as it contains the desired aura of mystery as far as the dog is concerned: if you do it properly, he doesn't know where the sensation imparted by your knee came from, and he therefore doesn't associate it with you.

people as well as your dog. Therefore, use the rod and spare the child.

If your dog jumps on you when the chain is not available, bring up your knee into his belly. He will not see the knee but will feel the sudden pain. When he goes down, praise him. It is far more pleasurable to be off you.

GO TO HEEL (OR) TAKING THE HEEL POSITION

The dog's instinct to hunt will cause him to follow an object that moves away from him. Therefore, place your dog in a Sit-Stay position in front of you. Hold the lead bunched up in your right hand. Say "**Go to heel**" and simultaneously take one step backward with your right foot. At the same moment snap lightly at the lead in the direction of your retreating leg. The dog instinctively will follow. When his head reaches your back leg, quickly bring the same leg forward along with your body momentum and, as you do this, switch the lead from your right hand to your left. Again the dog will follow the forward movement of your body. When he arrives at your left side, gently tug up on the lead, move your

Holding the lead bunched up in the right hand and taking a step backward with the right foot in teaching the dog to take the heel from the sitting position. (See additional sequential photos on pages 117 and 120.)

left hip into him and say "**Sit**." When he sits, he has completed the command. Praise lavishly and offer food.

The first inducement was the phrase "go to heel." Second was moving back with your right foot. Third was moving forward with your right foot. Fourth was leaning your hip into him. Fifth was snapping up on the lead. The food and praise served to confirm his response.

Repeat this training for 10 to 15 minutes. After several days, your dog should take the heel position when you say "**Go to heel**" without your having to move your body at all. No inducement other than the command will be necessary.

GO TO PLACE

Sometimes you want your dog to go to his place, to lie down and to stay there until you tell him he can leave. Obviously "going to place" on your dog's part will be a very valuable addition to his repertoire of learned commands.

To teach the command, put your dog in the automatic "sit" position at your side and stand approximately 3 feet away from the place you select as his destination. The place should be any location that is desirable for you. Hold the lead bunched up in your left hand. Say "**Place**" and simultaneously step in the direction of the place, snapping the lead in that direction and pointing your right hand in the same direction.

Move your right foot forward first, then your left in a dance-like rhythm; each time your right foot moves forward in the direction of the chosen place, simultaneously say "**Place**" and snap the lead in that direction. The rhythm should be "Place 2-3, Place 2-3, Place 2-3" etc., until you reach the de-

Teaching the dog to go to his place: the dog is in the sit position, while the teacher extends her right foot while pointing to the desired spot with the right hand, coincidentally snapping the lead in the same direction.

sired location, at which time you say "**Down**," using voice command and hand signal. When the dog goes down, praise him immediately and offer food. Then say "**Stay**" and leave him there for 2 to 3 minutes. If he tries to get up, rattle the chain and say "**Place**." If he starts to move, throw the chain at him, trying to strike his body anywhere from the neck down, and say "**Place**." If he continues to move, go after him and get hold of the lead at any expense. Then repeat the above procedure "Place, Place, Place," snapping the lead as before. Leave him in his place for 2 to 3 minutes.

Then call him to "**Come**." When he gets to you, praise him. Never tell him to do anything difficult for him to do (a command that he has not yet completely mastered, for example) after he comes to you. Coming to you should be followed only by pleasantries. Therefore, tell him to go to "**Heel**," which he already knows. After he responds, repeat "**Place**." Continue with this procedure 5 to 6 times, or until the dog responds to the "place" by pulling you there. When he does this, never hold him back. After he responds to the "place" 2 or 3 times, stop the lesson. No one is ever to bother him when he is in place. That is his place of comfort and rest. "Place" is not to be used as a negative command like "no." It is a positive command intended to let your dog know that it is time to get out of your way and for him to rest.

The following day, repeat the procedure from 3 feet away. After 2 or 3 successful attempts, when the dog responds on his own, move 3 or more feet farther back and repeat the same method. He will quickly pull you to place, and then it will be time for you to move 3 feet farther back, lengthening the distance after each successful mastery of a shorter distance.

The inducements are:
1. The word "place."
2. Stepping forward towards the place, thus using the dog's instinct to chase.
3. Snapping the lead in the direction of the place each time the word is uttered.
4. Praise and food rewards upon the arrival at the place, after he is made to lie down.

If the dog tries to leave his place, inducements to stay are:
1. Rattling of the throw chain.
2. Throwing the chain.

TEACHING TO COME

"Come" is probably the most important and essential of all obedience commands, since its proper execution can possibly save the life of your dog. Correct and immediate response to the "come" command may prevent him from darting out into the path of a passing vehicle or into other very real danger.

The errors so frequently made in the course of teaching this command result in precisely what we are trying to avoid. Instead of the dog hurrying to his master in a swift, joyful rush, the dog approaches timidly, hesitantly and even fearfully. He may even run in the opposite direction looking for a safe place to hide.

Never call a dog and then reprimand him for some previous act. The dog associates his coming to you only with the pain or pleasure you offer upon his arrival. When the dog comes to you, praise him, give him food, offer him affection and safety. If you sometimes offer positive reward and at other times offer discomfort, eventually the dog will become confused. He will never be certain whether this time he will be praised or punished. As a result, he might not come to you. If you chase him, he may seek a hiding place. I have seen dogs so confused that they have even snapped at the extended hand of the master simply out of fright. Biting is a dog's form of protecting himself. No dog bites unless he is doing so at the command of his master, is motivated to feel that he needs to protect himself or unless he is psychologically malformed. If there is nothing to fear, the dog will not bite. Where the dog fears the master we call this hand-shyness.

There are three types of shyness: genetic, man-caused, and environmental. A genetically shy dog is afraid of most unfamiliar people, places and things. The shyer he is, the greater is the fear he displays. This type of shyness can be cured only to a slight degree. This type of animal is generally not friendly toward strangers, but he can be a good pet in the right home.

The man-made shy dog can be helped through proper handling. However, it is certainly preferable to prevent this condition through proper handling from the beginning.

A dog that is environmentally shy can be helped by exposing him to those things in his environment that he is afraid of; once he realizes that they will not harm him, the condition will be resolved.

Regardless of your dog's temperament and how well you *think* he understands what he has done wrong, he doesn't speak or understand your language. When a correction is necessary, it must be executed at the *precise* moment of the misdeed—not five minutes later and not in anticipation of misconduct. Your success in training depends on how closely you are able to understand the modes of behavior which arise from his instincts.

Ever since the dog lived as a wild animal the pack instinct has been intrinsic. He has exercised a compulsion to remain in close association with his peers. His life with human beings, when he belongs to a family, resembles his life in a pack. A dog's dependence on man is but an expression of his pack instinct.

He suffers if he is left alone for any length of time. This is why I have some family member stay with Buddy when I must go out. It is because of his pack instinct that we are able to train the dog as opposed to, for instance, the cat, who is without a pack instinct. The cat requires stronger compulsions.

The dog in the family takes his place within the hierarchy of the human pack. He will most emphatically obey the pack leader. He will relate to or obey the other family members in direct proportion to their pack relationship. He may very well love and adore the three-year-old child, but he certainly will not be controlled by the youngster, for the infant is not capable of the enforcement of commands. His mental processes are not able to integrate the method of correction with its physical enforcement for a specific offense.

The stronger or bolder the dog, the stronger the leader must be—if he is to be the leader. A shy dog generally requires a lesser or weaker personality for a leader than does a highly spirited dog. A weak old man would have a far better marriage to a docile and submissive dog than he would to a bold one. Not everyone should own a dog. Before assuming the responsibility of owning such a pet it is vitally important that one understands that a dog is a sensitive living creature with feelings. He does not come out molded to his master's specifications. He is not a computer who instantly and automatically reacts to programmed data on command, which some individuals appear to seek when they take on the responsibility of a dog. Not everyone can own the same dog. Just as two nice people may not make it in marriage, they might each re-marry with positive results. The same is true with dog and man.

Buddy, in my opinion, is the boldest dog I have ever known. He fears nothing and has no hangups. Therefore, he is friendly to the world. However, not even the members of his family pack can control him to 85% efficiency. Each has control of him in direct proportion to their individual ability to concentrate, remain constant and enforce. One must never ask a dog to do anything unless it is wanted. But once you ask for it, you better get it. This doesn't mean to be cruel. It means one must be strong and offer love at the same time. Your ability to do this will decide what dog you can own and how well you can control him. This is of paramount importance and worthy of being repeated.

For example: Some people are more submissive by nature than others, and so are some dogs. When commanding a dog to sit, for example, if he doesn't comply instantly, the pack leader type of individual will repeat the command "Sit" and simultaneously enforce through the employment of prescribed compulsions, and he will apply the correction to the degree of intensity required to insure 100% and instant response. Upon the dog's taking of the sit position the man is to offer lavish praise and/or food reward and is to be sincere in offering the reinforced praising.

The dog who is bold or of pack leadership quality will be quick to know that his owner is not strong by the nature of the owner's attitude and means of enforcement. The submissive type of individual might, for example, ask his dog to "sit" in a weak I-don't-really-expect-to-be-obeyed tone, and when the dog doesn't respond, the owner's attitude will remain a request and not a command. The bold dog requires a leader stronger in character than that of his own. If such is not the case, and if the owner is not capable of learning to be more dominant, surely he would be far better off owning a timid bitch than a bold male like Buddy. The dog must respect the physical abilities of his pack leader. Dogs don't regard owners incapable of enforcement to be true pack leaders. This does not mean that the pack leader must be rough or crude. It simply means that he must get whatever he commands 100% of the time; the methods he is to employ in gaining this despotic control are spelled out in this book.

To expand, a nine-year-old would certainly have a far better chance of attaining the role of pack leader with a submissive female miniature Poodle than with a bold male Doberman Pinscher. You simply can't own a dog who doesn't believe that you are capable of leadership. Both dogs and owners are better off when the requirements of both are matched according to temperament and size.

There are some distractions that will cause the dog to leave his master's side. He may see a passing vehicle, a fleeing cat, or a rabbit running. After he successfully or unsuccessfully consummates his chase, he will return to the pack leader—you. Since we don't want to join him in his hunt, as his animal pack leader would, it is essential that he learn to come unfailingly, regardless of the distraction presented. Within the animal pack, the leader has despotic power, and all the other dogs are subordinate to him. The human being takes the place of the pack leader. The dog is undoubtedly content to be absolutely subordinate to him, provided inducements and compulsions are imposed with the same unwavering despotic force that would be imposed by the dog pack leader. But even a good leader-subordinate relationship does not insure special performance such as coming when there is overwhelming distraction. Such obedience has to be learned.

Whenever I take a strange dog for training, the very first thing I do is to affectionately pat him, offer him food and then attach him to a 3-foot stall chain. After about half an hour passes, I take him outside onto the street for a pleasurable walk. I am certain to offer him this sort of relationship before training begins—this is when it has become obviously clear that he has accepted me as his new and temporary leader. If I were to start to physically force or compel him without first establishing a dog-pack relationship—his finished work could never be animated happiness. You can do almost anything with a dog once you are his accepted friend and leader.

The dog must always be given a positive and agreeable experience as well as a friendly reception when he arrives at his master's side. Therefore, if your dog does something wrong, don't call him with the intention of making a correction on his arrival. Once you call him and he arrives, only offer positive reinforcement.

In dealing with a dog in a conditioning or teaching context, we must consider the pleasure or displeasure we are offering by our acts and the proper apportionment of positive and negative experiences. Dogs exhibit certain distinctive modes of behavior, for example the pack instinct or fear-biting, which I term "compulsions." We must break these so-called "compulsions" by designating a certain command to which the dog *must* respond and then finding a mode of enforcement.

We never start to work with a dog unless he is devoid of depression. The dog must be happy and in good spirits if he is to learn with a positive attitude. This can be accomplished by the human pack leader's temporarily transforming himself into a playful pack companion of equal rank. This interchange of roles is an important matter to the dog. The changeover from pack leader to pack companion will bring the instinct of play into operation at once. To perform this act, you are to make short, jerky body movements going to and fro, as if making turns, playful attacks or attempts at flight. One should behave as dogs themselves do at play. This kind of play is also motivated by the utterance

Establishing the mood prior to a training session is important. Dogs, like people, have their ups and downs in temperament, and it is much better to put the dog into a responsive frame of mind for training than to ignore his temperamental barometer. The better you simulate the actions of dogs at play in a pack, the better you'll succeed in setting the mood. Don't worry about looking or feeling foolish. . . get in there and have a good romp with your friend. You'll both be the better for it.

of play call in a high pitched voice. For example, long, drawn out repetitions of "goooood puppy." This will have a most stimulating effect.

The uninformed may consider this type of playful carrying on with the animal ridiculous. But our aim is to establish good understanding between man and dog, and this can only be achieved by initially putting ourselves on the same level with the animal.

A dog must learn to do what is required in response to audible or visible signals. For this purpose, right from the start, a certain sound should be made at the same time the dog feels the snapping of the lead and hears the word "come."

Before starting any training session, attach the dog to the 3-foot stall chain for at least 15 minutes. He will be happy when you release him and start your outdoor walk. If he is not in good spirits, dogplay with him. Also, make certain that he hasn't eaten for several hours prior to training. Let him be hungry. Thus, when you offer the food reward after he comes to you, it will be more meaningful and communication will take place more quickly and be more effective.

Before beginning the training session, examine the prong or spiked collar. Be certain that it is fitted around the dog's neck so that when you snap the lead he will feel the constriction of the prongs. If the collar is too tight, you will not be able to snap the lead effectively. If the collar is too loose, when you snap the lead he will not feel the prongs.

When you begin on your walk, allow the dog to first eliminate. This is pleasurable and relaxing to him. Keep him on the lead while he excretes. Praise him after he finishes, and continue on your joyful walk, always maintaining a good, jovial attitude. Stop walking and put him through those commands he has already learned. Do this briefly, and with fun. The dog will now be in a working frame of mind. His instinct for pack membership will be rekindled. Review his already-learned commands for several minutes; when you see he is in high spirits (for he clearly understands and so is pleasing his human pack leader) it is time to start the new command.

Put your dog in a "sit-stay" or "down-stay" position while on the six foot lead. The psychological state of the dog when left away from his master in the "down"position is one of submission mixed with loneliness. The sit position will arouse loneliness, too. The trainer, as he walks away, arouses the impulse in the animal to rejoin his master. This im-

With the dog in the sit position, the trainer snaps his fingers and offers verbal encouragement while stepping backwards, providing an impetus for the dog to follow. (See pages 125 and 128 for other photos showing how to teach the dog to come.)

pulse grows as the distance and period of absence lengthen. It is a happy release for the dog when he is able, in accordance with the pack instinct, to rejoin his master. The psychological state of the dog, when left alone, affords an excellent opportunity for obtaining an enthusiastic and happy reaction when rejoining his human pack master. Therefore, say "**Come**" in a positive and soft voice. Simultaneously snap your fingers, and as you do so, gently snap the lead toward you, which will induce the dog to stand and "come"; at the same moment, start to step quickly backwards. The dog will want to rejoin you, for your act of stepping backwards caters to his hunting instincts as well as his pack instinct, encouraging happy response. Upon arrival, offer the dog lavish praise and food as a reward. This cannot be said too often. Repeat this performance for 15 to 20 minutes. He will quickly learn that upon the command "come" it is far more pleasurable to rejoin his pack leader than to stay away and feel even the slightest discomfort aroused by gentle jerking of the lead.

Be certain that you offer genuine praise in a high-pitched voice, as well as food when the dog rejoins or reaches you. Repeat this exercise for a few days until the dog clearly understands and performs perfectly. You cannot attempt to begin off-lead "come" until the on-lead work is perfect. If the dog breaks from his "down-stay" position in anticipation of your saying "**Come**," you must correct him the instant he starts to move. Say "**No**" and lightly toss the throw chain so it strikes his chest. He will quickly stop his forward motion. As he does so, praise him and allow him to remain in the sit or down position for several minutes. Then call him and induce him to sit automatically when he arrives in front of you. This is done very simply by taking one quick step in toward the dog as he approaches you. Stand tall, gently snap the lead upward and simultaneously say "**Sit**." Your moving into him will induce him to stop moving forward. By snapping the lead up he will be compelled to sit; again praise him lavishly and offer food when he reacts properly. Repeat this exercise for several days. Soon the dog will respond to come and, upon reaching you, he will automatically sit without audio or visual inducement. Be certain not to give the "down" command after the dog comes. "Down" is a strong compulsion. When he "comes" the dog should experience only fun and positive reinforcement. Therefore, after you finish with your praise say "**Heel**" and continue with your merry walk around the neighborhood.

End each training session only after the dog has correctly responded two or three times without correction. Then say "**Okay**," signifying freedom, and begin the dog pack play for several minutes. Very quickly the word "okay" will come to mean dog pack play, fun and freedom.

After the dog has reached the point of 100% response to your "come" command on the lead, you can now move on toward achieving the real intended goal. The dog should come off the lead to his master instantly and happily in response to the hand signal or voice command regardless of the intensity of the distraction. Thus far, the type of compulsion we have employed is not strong enough to offer the protection we are seeking from strong distractions such as a passing car.

Now that the dog is happily coming to you as a result of having invariably enjoyed pleasurable experiences on making his approach, the most effective means for reinforcement of the word "come" would be some method which would enable us to offer fright, however distant the dog might be. The moment the feeling of fright begins and ceases, a caressing "come" should be said, and as soon as the frightened animal looks at its master, the man should run backward and repeat the word "come." If the dog should show hesitancy in responding, the man could go down into a crouching position on his knees or even lying flat, chest down on the floor, and repeat "**Come**." The crouching or lying position affords friendship and safety to the dog as opposed to the alarm or danger he would have just experienced. With these inducements the dog, even if exposed to the most intense distraction, will learn to put them aside and run to his master. This will eliminate all the difficulties connected with the achievement of a reliable response to "come."

The problem then becomes one of finding something to substitute for the imaginary car. What can we use? The first expedient is the use of a long lead about 20 to 30 feet long. Do with this long lead as you did with the short one. From the "down-stay" or "sit-stay" position, tell your dog to "come." As you do so, snap the lead to you and run backward. When he reaches you, praise him lavishly and offer food. Repeat this exercise for fifteen to twenty minutes for as many days as are necessary for your dog to come without your having to snap the lead. You might be pleasantly surprised to find that after only one session you no longer have to snap the lead. After this has been achieved, move to an enclosed area such as a fenced in yard or school yard or playground. This is done to insure safety. Allow the dog to run freely with the long lead attached to his collar. When his attention is not on you, say "**Come**" and simultaneously toss the throw chain at him and step on the lead. Be certain that he is not looking at you when you throw the chain. The sound and striking of the chain against his body will initiate fear but no physical pain. As he jolts away, the constricting of the prongs around his neck caused by your stepping on the lead, coordinated with the sound "come" and your crouching, will induce him to run away from his fright and to you, his pack leader, for safety. Repeat this exercise until you reach the point at which your dog responds the moment you say "**Come**." Once he does so, take off the lead and repeat the exercise. Say "**Come**" when his attention is elsewhere and merely rattle the chain. If he responds, praise him lavishly. If he doesn't respond, repeat the exercise but now throw the chain at the dog instead of just rattling it. Repeat this until the dog comes on command without use of the chain.

Some dogs possess a strong pack leader instinct and a weak pack instinct. This type of animal will possibly be more interested in challenging another dog than in joining you, his pack leader. His nature is more independent than that of dogs possessing strong pack instincts, so to insure his safety from potential danger it is necessary to utilize stronger inducements.

The method I use is perhaps painful to dog and dog lover, but it is far more kind than to allow the dog to be killed by a passing automobile. This is to use a slingshot as a deterrent. I am describing this method only as a last resort, and a few things should be emphatically impressed on the reader's mind before he goes any further. *The slingshot is the most extreme form of correction ever to be used.* Of the literally thousands of dogs I have trained, I have very seldom been forced to resort to this method. Generally, the milder corrections are sufficient,

The stage is set for the forbidden action, in this case garbage-eating. In order to get the idea into the dog's mind that he should associate the forbidden action with an immediate and never-failing unpleasant response, you have absolutely no choice but to keep an active watch over the dog when he is in the situation that could lead to his misbehaving. Then you must make your correction—whether it be throwing the throw chain or tin can filled with marbles or using the slingshot or other deterrent—immediately upon his performance of the action that you don't want him to perform. He cannot be allowed to get away with it even just once in a while, so you have to stay on top of the situation, even if it means that you have to keep a steady hours-long watch over him. You are trying to psyche the dog into believing that there is some natural force at work in the world that immediately punishes garbage-eating dogs. The more mysterious the whole process is to him, the better he'll learn his lesson, because dogs don't question mysterious processes; they just learn to avoid their consequences. Your object is to convince the dog that garbage-eating or whatever other bad habit you're trying to break him of is ALWAYS and IMMEDIATELY followed by something unpleasant for him. Once he associates the forbidden action with a certain unpleasant consequence, he'll stop doing the action.

especially if your dog loves you—which he certainly should. If you find it necessary to resort to the slingshot method, you must first practice your aim with the slingshot for from two to four weeks. If you can perfect it, fine. If not, you must employ the assistance of a professional whose aim is sure.

Now, have someone walk outside the fence with a dog. Allow your dog to run freely. Say "**Come**" and, using the slingshot, simultaneously shoot your dog with a pebble. If the pebble doesn't work, use a marble. Make certain the shot strikes the dog on his body anywhere from the neck down; avoid the head at all costs. Immediately crouch and say "**Come**." When the dog gets to you, praise him lavishly and offer food. After two or three successful shots, your dog will respond as soon as he hears the sound "come." To my way of reasoning, any dog owner would prefer to use the slingshot several times, if necessary, than to take the chance of a car crushing his dog. The problem involved with use of the slingshot as a corrective device arises from the degree of impracticality connected with its use—most people simply are not good at hitting things with it—not from any defect in the method itself. It really is no more "cruel" to employ a slingshot as a last-resort method of correction than it is to deprive a dog of food to keep its weight down. I have found over the years that in many cases the people who register the most ostensible outrage over the use of the slingshot to train the otherwise uncorrectable dog are exactly the ones who show the greatest degree of insensitivity to their pets' requirements—and in many cases they unknowingly or unthinkingly subject their animals to gross *real* cruelty. I once had an experience, for example, with a woman who berated me for even bringing up the topic of using the slingshot method on her recalcitrant pet—and all the while her poor dog was stifling in her car parked in full sunlight with the windows rolled up on a broiling hot day. Did she mean to be cruel? Of course not—but she had subjected the dog to an agonizing experience nonetheless, and I have no idea how many times she's done the same thing, or something equally callous, since.

My intent is not to punish a dog unnecessarily or cause him needless pain, but simply to educate him, and I know of no other method as effective as the slingshot.

Not until the trainer has learned how to allot pleasantness and unpleasantness in correct proportion will he satisfy one of the principal requirements for creating an understanding between man and dog. This applies throughout the entire course of training. True expertise in meting out "rewards" and "punishments" will come only with experience, because you have to develop a feel for what you're doing before you can recognize the fine edge of response. In training a dog you are dealing with a being capable of intelligent action and emotion, you're not dealing with purely physical and easily measurable quantities. Training a dog involves a lot of give and take between him and you and to a good extent requires mutual trust and respect. You're not ladling an exact three ounces of sugar into a bowl for a cake recipe or figuring how many square feet of plywood you have to buy to cover a hole in a floor. Those calculations are easy because they are easy to grasp and measure, whereas dog training has to do with the application of factors that are, unfortunately, not definable by yardstick or scale.

Special Problems

PREVENTING UNWANTED CHEWING

You know that you should catch the dog in the act of the undesirable behavior in order to effectively employ the throw chain. Therefore, when you are not present to supervise, prevent the pleasurable chewing act by keeping the animal in an enclosed area (even a cage) so as to prevent the pleasurable experience. If the dog is not allowed to experience pleasure through chewing and instead feels the chain each time he does chew, he will receive no pleasure but rather discomfort and will understand. If he still manages to chew, he will have accomplished the chewing because he outsmarted you, the master. At this point the only other remedy is to put the article he chewed into his mouth and tie his mouth, forcing him to endure this displeasure for 20 minutes or longer. If you were forced to keep your favorite food in your mouth without swallowing for 20 minutes, you would probably regurgitate. The dog will feel the same way. However, if his need to chew is stronger than your compulsion for him not to chew, he will continue to chew. Therefore, prevent him from chewing by recognizing what causes him to chew in the first place and then eliminate the thing that causes him to chew.

There are various reasons why dogs chew. If the impetuses are eliminated, the chewing problems can be arrested.

A. *Worms:* Worm parasites steal the nutritive value of the dog's food, forcing it to chew in an effort to satisfy nutritional needs. Physical signs of worms are:

1. Running eyes
2. Potbelly
3. Coughing
4. Insatiable appetite
5. Loose bowel movement
6. Poor coat—dandruff
7. Skinny and bony appearance

If you bring a stool specimen from the dog to your veterinarian, he will be able to determine whether parasites exist and, if they do, will eliminate the problem through treatment.

B. *Teething in young puppies:* Provide a pacifier such as a Nylon bone as a substitute to chew on on.

C. *Insecurity.* This is a common cause for chewing. The best thing to do is either prevent the problem by caging the dog or provide a substitute toy, such as a Nylon bone, to chew. Very often the dog will adopt this sort of toy as a puppy child, and the problem will be eliminated. Leaving on a radio playing soothing music or steady talk will help.

D. Dogs who chew plaster walls or porous things very often do so to help overcome a physiological problem—namely an over-secretion of gastric juices. An antacid will overcome this problem. Almost every dog outgrows the chewing problem. Some will outgrow it at 6 months, some at 1 year, some at 18 months and some at 2½ years of age. When people do something that is socially highly unacceptable we incarcerate them. It is a lot kinder to put a dog in a cage whenever we can't watch him

Sometimes dogs, puppies especially, chew on things their owners don't want them to chew on simply because they don't have anything more pleasant to chew on. For dogs in that category, owners can often solve the problem by providing a substitute chewable item that the dog will derive pleasure from, such as the hambone-flavored Nylon bone (sold in pet shops under the name Nylabone) shown being chewed here.

than it is to give him away. The next party may not be willing to put up with the problem, and who knows where the dog will wind up. If you are not willing to sacrifice, you shouldn't own a dog to begin with. Certainly a cage is not much of a sacrifice if all other methods fail.

Garbage Stealing: Again, the best method of correction is prevention. If you don't have garbage lying around there can't be any problem. If you must keep the garbage around, set things up so that you can catch the dog in the act of approaching the garbage, and then throw the chain. If you catch him each time that he makes his attempt, naturally he will get the message.

If a combination of outwitting the dog, judicious use of the throw chain or elimination of the trouble's cause doesn't cure stool-eating and chewing problems, the quickest and surest—albeit drastic—method is to use the slingshot technique. In employing the slingshot technique, the situation must be set up so that the dog is not aware of the trainer's presence. For example, stool is left in the yard and the dog is set free. The trainer is hiding on the roof. The moment the dog attempts to eat the stool, the trainer shoots the dog with a marble. The dog's head should be such that there is no danger of hitting his eyes. If you are not certain of your aim, don't use the slingshot. Two or three well-aimed shots will almost always correct stool-eating as well as the chewing problem. The slingshot method is the sure-fire method, but it of course must be used with great care.

Housebreaking and Paper Breaking

Dogs are never ever housebroken or paper-broken. Rather, they are "spot broken," so to speak. First you teach your dog to excrete on a piece of newspaper situated in a particular area of your home. Each time he excretes at the desired location you praise him. Each time he misses the spot you reprimand him. Finally he gets the idea and goes only on the paper. Then you decide you want to housebreak him, so you remove the paper. The dog quite naturally returns to the spot where the paper had previously been. Now when he takes care of his needs, you scold him. As a result, he may become confused. He may start to think it is wrong to excrete, and when you walk him in the street he will hold back for fear of being punished.

No dog should be paper broken if you are going to eventually housebreak him. A young puppy who is not ready for housebreaking should be allowed to excrete in some isolated area without having any fuss or attention given to this natural act. After the puppy excretes, the waste should be cleaned immediately. A dog is ready to start being housebroken when he is physically capable of walking. However, he should not be taken into the street until he has received permanent DHL inoculations. He must be 12 weeks of age in order for his body to accept permanent immunity. Therefore, we start housebreaking at this point.

The normally alert and intelligent friendly dog is one that is best for training of any kind, and in order for a dog to be truly responsive to the demands made on him by training he has to be in good health; a sick dog cannot perform at his best. Therefore you want to make sure that your dog is in good health before beginning any training program. Photo by Louise van der Meid.

Before starting housebreaking, you must make certain that your dog is healthy. He should be physically well and have no parasites. If he has worms he will have a loose stool and will not be able to hold his movement. Also, the dog can have no physiological problems relating to the digestive or excretory systems. He must be in good health before housebreaking starts.

DIET

To housebreak any dog, the first thing to be considered is his diet. It must be regulated. You must feed him the same food at the same time every day. If you vary his food intake or the times of feeding, you will vary his digestive process, and logically it follows that his excretory process will become irregular. Therefore, you must feed him the same thing at the same time every day, ensuring consistency of digestive and excretory systems. If your dog turns up his nose at the food, leave it there for ten minutes. If he doesn't eat, take it away and save the food for his next feeding. When the dog becomes hungry enough, he will eat. Dogs can go without eating for much longer than you'd think, so don't let him con you into giving him food at irregular intervals. He will eat when he is hungry. The diet you feed your dog really should depend on the individual animal's system. Just like people, each dog is an individual; what one dog does well with, another might not. However, I will proceed to tell you the diet I have found to work beautifully with the many dogs I have worked with.

In a pressure cooker, preferably, although a regular pot can be used, put an equal amount of water and rice. First just put in the water; after it boils, add the rice. The quantity to be made depends upon how often and how much you feed your dog. Few dogs should get less than one-half a handful of cooked rice, and few should get more than two handfuls at each feeding. To the pot, add a diced up raw carrot and raw celery stalk. To this add several marrow bones. After a few minutes, all the water will be gone.

Every dog needs carbohydrates, or starch, which the rice provides. Every dog needs minerals from the carrot and celery. Every animal requires protein to build body tissue. The marrow bone provides this. Put in anywhere from one-half a handful to two handfuls of the cooked rice in a clean dish. To this add hard-boiled egg, one or two daily. This is a great source of additional protein. Never use a raw egg, for it will pass through the dog's system without being digested. To the rice-egg-marrow bone concoction, add boiled chicken or, in some cases, various types of commercially prepared dry foods. Again, it all depends on what you and your veterinarian determine to be the needs of your individual animal. If it is too much trouble or if time won't permit cooking each day, you can cook for the entire week and keep the food covered and refrigerated. At each feeding just take out what you need.

Every puppy needs calcium to build bones and teeth. However, he cannot assimilate calcium unless he gets vitamin D with it. So add one, two and in some cases even more calcium pills, depending upon the size and needs of the individual animal. One cod liver oil capsule should provide all the vitamin D necessary. Consult your veterinarian for his opinion as to how much calcium to feed your pet.

To dogs (puppies) with very sensitive stomachs I give pot cheese and eggs and boiled chicken. Dogs with stronger stomachs can do well on some of the commercially prepared foods.

Never give table food to your dog when attempting to housebreak. Table food has spices that can irritate the walls of the canine digestive tract, causing loose stools and thus making it impossible for the dog to hold.

The water intake should be regulated as well. If water is left available all day, the dog will drink out of habit, not need. He will pass the water dish and lick at it all day. Therefore, he will have to urinate all day. Also, too much water is not healthy. It will stop the stomach from secreting an enzyme necessary for proper digestion. The dog should be watered two times daily. In the morning—after breakfast, he should be given a full dish of water. If he wants more, give it to him. When he stops drinking, take it away. At night, after dinner, do the same. A dog's excessive drinking might be a sign of some physiological problem. Have it checked out. If your dog has just finished exercising and is very hot and seems to be very thirsty—don't give him water. If you do, it can kill him. No animal should drink when overheated. Give him an ice cube to quench his thirst.

A healthy dog should excrete a well shaped solid stool. If your dog doesn't, something is wrong. A new diet may cause loose movements for several days. However, if the stool continues to be non-formed, have your vet offer an opinion. A poorly shaped excretion is an indication of some problem which must be treated.

Dogs are natural cave dwellers. What we humans refer to as a clean dog is one who would leave his cave, urinate and defecate and then return to his cave. What we refer to as a dirty dog is one who will excrete in his cave and lie in it. Many dogs are dirty because of improper care during the first six weeks of their lives. Their living quarters were not properly cleaned or cared for. These pups urinate and defecate and are forced to remain in their own excretion.

Lying in excrement eventually becomes pleasurable for them, and the pleasure is of a distinctly sensual type, perhaps even sexual. If forced to lie in their own excrement, some dogs get to like the sensation very much and seek out whatever gratification they derive from it whenever they can. Various theories have been advanced to account for the actions of a dog that rolls around in its own excrement. . . some say the warmth of the excrement is the attractant, some say the combination of warmth and moistness, some say that there is a definite sexual connotation. Whatever the underlying reason or reasons, I know from personal observation that some dogs unquestionably are dirty dogs in the strict sense that they wallow in fecal matter and give every evidence of relishing their actions while they do it. To the degree that a dog's owner occasions the practice by *forcing* the dog into its obviously pleasurable association with feces, such a dog is a man-made creation.

Other dogs may have physiological problems and therefore may resort to eating their own as well as other animals' eliminations. The stool eating problem generally resolves itself when the dog reaches maturity. Regardless, a dirty dog is one who will lie in his own excretion. The so-called clean dog is easier or generally requires less effort to housebreak.

Whenever an animal excretes, he experiences pleasure. If he is prevented from experiencing this pleasure when indoors and has the pleasure of excretion only when outdoors, he will want to hold his excretion until he gets onto the street. However, if he excretes indoors and goes uncorrected just as when excreting outside, he will continue to go in both places. Therefore, we make use of the clean dog's natural ways. When we can't watch him, we keep him in a cave-like situation, thus preventing accidents. A cage is excellent for this purpose. If a cage is not available, a short stall chain will suffice. Attach the dog to the end of the chain. The clean dog will try to hold when placed in this situation. If he doesn't, shorten the chain or get a smaller cage. Let the dog free only when you can watch him. If he excretes say "**NO**" and toss the chain at him. The pleasurable experience of excretion will become a non-pleasurable experience. If each time the dog is caught and corrected during an indoor act of excretion, and if he is praised each time he excretes outdoors, he will quickly become conditioned. If you

The cage is the best available simulation available to satisfy a dog's normal craving for a cave-like atmosphere. A cage is excellent for preventing indoor excretion by the naturally clean dog, for while he is confined in his cage he will have a natural aversion to soiling it, making it easier for his owner to be prepared to take him to his proper station outdoors. Unfortunately, the cage is not an effective conditioning instrument when dealing with the dirty dog—whether the dog is a naturally dirty dog or a man-made dirty dog—because forcing him into proximity with his excretions is for such a dog a pleasant, not unpleasant, experience.

don't catch him in the act, you cannot correct him. No association will be made. By keeping the naturally clean dog tied to the chain or inside the cage, we prevent him from having pleasurable experiences indoors.

If your pet is what we refer to as a dirty dog, however, the cage and/or short chain won't work. In such cases, you have two choices. The first is to keep the dog outside constantly so that he goes only outside. He will become conditioned in this way. Then, when you take him indoors, watch him constantly and have your throw chain ready to use. The second choice is to watch the dirty dog around the clock, so that each time he eliminates, he experiences negative conditioning. He receives your praise

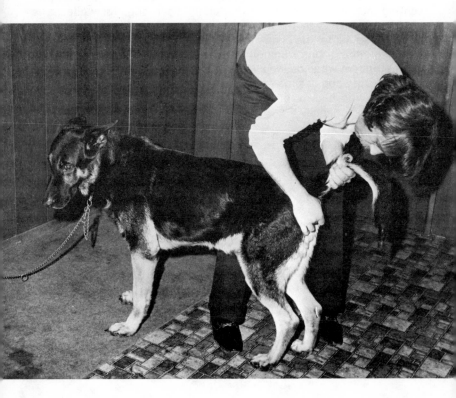

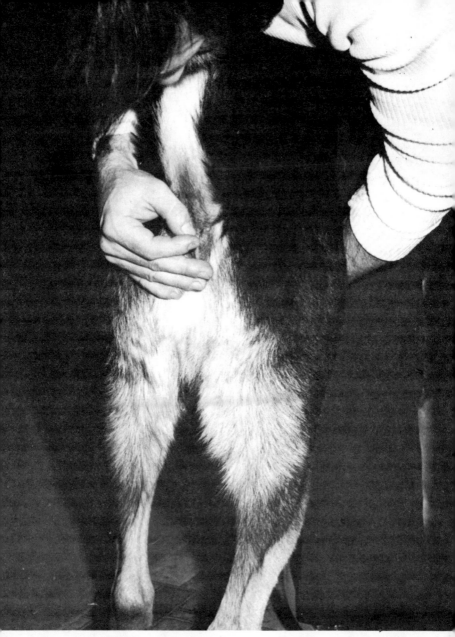

Above and opposite: Rear and side views of steps in the process of administering a suppository into the dog's rectum to induce defecation. The purpose of inducing defecation is to have a good control over the point in time at which the dog will defecate so that you can be there to award praise for doing the job in the right place. See color photos on page 124 outlining the entire process of inducing outdoor defecation.

only when he excretes outdoors. You will also find that contrary to what many people surmise, the cage is not cruel. After several days of living in the cage, if the cage door is left open, the dog will return to the cage of his own will. This will become his cave and so a place of security.

Some dogs present the problem of not excreting when outdoors. The reasons can be timidness, man created hangups, or just not knowing what is expected or why. For those dogs, we use a suppository to induce excretion. After defecation, generally urination will follow. If the suppository doesn't prove to be successful, use a warm water enema. After several inducements, the dog will feel comfortable when excreting outdoors and will understand what is expected.

Excessive urination might be a symptom of cystitis. If such a condition exists, have your vet treat the dog. Generally, after a relatively short treatment the infection will be gone and housebreaking can continue.

WALKING PROCEDURE

The dog must know that he can depend upon you, his pack leader, to walk him at regularly scheduled hours. Dogs who eat more frequently (puppies) have to be walked more often. Puppies on three or four feedings a day should be walked the first thing in the morning—as soon as you get out of bed and again immediately after breakfast. Again, three to four hours later. You should also walk the dog immediately after lunch and immediately after dinner. Always walk the dog before you go to sleep. Remember this: you can never walk the dog too often. As he matures, he will become stronger and better able to contain himself. Also, he will be eating less frequently, so he'll require fewer walks. A puppy on three or four feedings should get six to eight walks in 24 hours. A puppy given two feedings (one approximately six months old) should be given five to seven walks. A puppy on one feeding (ten months or older) generally can get by with three walks in a 24-hour period. Regardless of age, every dog should be walked at a *minimum* of three times each day.

To summarize: if the dog is fed the same thing at the same time every day, his digestive system will be regulated and so will his excretory system. If he is prevented from excreting indoors and eliminates only when outdoors, outdoor elimination will become the conditioned habit. If he does excrete inside and is caught in the act and immediately corrected, his experience will not be pleasurable. So, if he can rely on you, his master, to walk him at regularly scheduled hours, he will become housebroken. Paper breaking is a much simpler task. If a dog, be he clean or dirty, is kept tied in one area or is constantly left in a cage, he has no choice but to excrete there. Each time he does so, he experiences the delight of elimination. If you let him free, watch him; if he excretes, toss the chain saying "**NO.**" He will quickly get the idea.

It is important for the novice to understand that the most housebroken of dogs is capable of urinating or defecating in the house at various times. A sick dog cannot hold. A dog with diarrhea cannot hold. Even healthy dogs will eliminate. Going back to the dog pack, remember that in the wild dogs excrete to mark off territorial rights and to let potential mates know of their presence. Before going to sleep, dogs will mark off territory by urinating, thereby telling other animals to keep away.

When we bring the dog into our house and domesticate him, so to speak, as far as he is concerned your home is his territory. If he doesn't urinate or defecate at various times, he will have an anal secretion which you describe as a doggy odor. If he smells a near-by female in season—even a human female—he may urinate. (Some dogs have been known to urinate on the master's side of the matress or mistress's side. What he is doing is sexually claiming. A male dog may select the master or mistress and a female dog might do the same. All dogs are bi-sexual.)

When you walk a stud male dog on the street, he will pick his leg up at each tree or fire pump, regardless of whether he has to urinate or not. What he is doing is sexually marking off territory, leaving his calling card. Therefore, understand that your dog is a living thing, not a machine. He has emotions and sensitivities and is driven sexually like yourself. His occasional household urinary excretions should be understood. If not, you shouldn't own a dog.

Protection Work

Opinions differ as to what constitutes a guard dog and what an attack dog. This diversity is caused partly by the variability of requirements for each classification; to a certain extent, they overlap.

If you were walking down the street with your dog and someone offered verbal abuse or any type of danger that the dog was not aware of but you were—upon your verbal command the dog should show aggression. He should bark vigorously and appear as if he were going to rip up the potential criminal, but if he were to be set free, he would not bite. Upon a second verbal command he should instantly stop barking. This is a guard dog.

If he were an attack dog, after learning guard work he would have been taught to bite using the full strength of his body weight, force and momentum. Again, upon command he would stop biting instantly and hold the criminal at bay. If the criminal remained motionless, the dog would just observe him. If the criminal offered movement, the dog would resume his attack automatically and continue to bite until commanded to stop or until the criminal became motionless. Also, if someone were to attack the master, the dog would attack the criminal automatically, requiring no command, and be called off upon the master's oral signal. A *genuine* attack dog can work off lead in all situations. If he is a dog who protects a home or a business or any establishment where people come and go unescorted or uninvited, he should remain neutral or be friendly to strangers unless commanded to show aggression by a mature member of his pack. If left alone, he should bark at strangers and attack on his own if necessary. A naturally friendly and good-humored dog who can be turned into a hostile one upon signal is a very valuable family dog. Timid dogs are always suspicious and often display their temperament by indiscriminately barking at strangers, sometimes backing away as they do so. These animals are hostile and have been known to bite without due cause. This type of dog belongs in a situation where the doors are kept locked and strangers enter only upon personal escort by a mature pack member capable of controlling the animal. They can be used in yard situations to scare off potential intruders and to protect enclosed property, but they are otherwise unreliable.

No dog who works with man should ever be taught to use his attacking equipment unless he is first taught complete obedience and not unless he has a genuine pack leader capable of 100% control and leadership. An uncontrollable gun is of no value to anyone; worse, it's highly dangerous.

Dogs who are frightened or who are fear biters should not be taught to attack. If the master is not alert, these dogs are capable of using their equipment indiscriminately out of fear. It is the feeling of the author that attack dogs should be registered, and not everyone should be allowed to own one. A properly trained attack dog with good temperament in the hands of a sensible adult who is capable of 100% obedience control and also of being 100% pack leader is not neurotic and is a family protector as well as loving companion. No dog ever turns on his true master, his real pack leader. He merely challenges for leadership, and an attack–trained dog is no more likely to challenge for leadership than the

Don't make the mistake of thinking that a naturally nasty-tempered dog makes the best type of animal to train for attack work. For attack work the best dog to use is the naturally friendly and outgoing dog, which is more likely to be much braver in a pinch than the dog that's always snarling. The snarling dog often is a basically scared animal that covers up its underlying fearful disposition with an outward show of bravado. The friendly animal also is more responsive and amenable to training. Photo by Louise van der Meid.

so-called household pet. The important thing is that each dog have a genuine pack leader controlling him.

Training for attack work may be undertaken either exclusively with fictitious malefactors in ordinary clothing or with assistants in protective clothing. The latter would certainly be inadequate training for the real thing, since the dog would be conditioned to pay attention mainly to the protective clothing and would remain indifferent to persons in ordinary clothes. Therefore, when training is carried out in protective clothing, other people in ordinary street clothes must also take part. They should not be used, however, until the dog is absolutely *perfect* when commanded to leave the bite. This is *complete* submissiveness—an indispensable quality in this type of training. If complete submissiveness is not perfected before using people in ordinary clothing, the people are in danger. Because of the great excitement of the animal when attacking, getting him to stop instantly upon command requires far greater submissiveness than any obedience work and in reality will make you a stronger pack leader and your dog a happier one.

Protective clothing also offers advantages which cannot be under-rated. The dog can practice actual seizing from the beginning, and the trainer will have many opportunities to employ the release command. The procedure will be carried out so that the dog will go after one specific spot on the sleeve or protective suit; he will be induced to do so by the criminal stand-in's backing away, which inspires the dog to chase. It will become a game to the dog if done correctly. The assistant acting as the criminal should not be changed until biting has been learned. This will enable the dog to make most rapid progress. In all training the fictitious criminal must be seen by the dog at the very beginning of each session. We never move on to using a man without protective clothing until complete control of the dog is certain in all situations when using protective clothing, and when we move on to a man in street clothes it should be done in a different setting, a place where the former work has never been carried out. As training advances, both locations and assistants should be constantly changed. Companionship between the trainer and his dog, when doing aggressive training, will rapidly grow and will lead to the closest association of both within the pack. The dog's confidence, dependence and submissiveness when called upon to cease with the bite will be won

The value of the protective sleeve becomes obvious when you consider the biting power of a large dog; even with the sleeve protecting his arm, the "criminal" can sometimes feel the pressure of the dog's jaws. Here (above) the dog has been taunted and has begun to leave his master's side in an approach to the taunter, displaying canine displeasure all the way; below, he has seized the sleeve and is doing his best to ravage it.

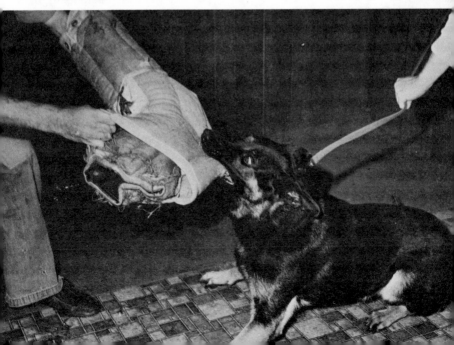

The person simulating the criminal should feign a combination of sneakiness and cowardice; he should skulk into the room rather than enter in a normal manner, and once he's in he should perform furtively in all his actions. He should be especially good at feigning fright, thereby encouraging the dog to become bolder in resisting his annoyances and threats. He should be coaxed into emitting little squeals of terror and should be coached into scurrying away rather than just retreating at the advance of the dog.

in a very short time. Another advantage is that the dog's aggressive spirit will continue to grow as the exercise continues.

Protection work can be carried out while the dog is learning obedience, but it is a good idea, especially in the case of novice trainers and with timid dogs, not to do so until obedience has been mastered. In the case of professionals, both can be carried out within the same general time span but at different intervals.

BARK ON COMMAND

To start with this type of work, one should select an environment with which the dog is completely familiar. He will be more ready to defend himself against human beings when he feels safe in his environment and has his master next to him. The farther away the trainer/pack leader is, the weaker the dog's defensive instinct becomes. The trainer should be at the side of the dog.

A dog within his pack is more strong than the animal who is alone. We move to strange environments only after the dog is strong in his own domain. A dog in a kennel, if handled properly, will become a pack member and will feel secure in the kennel area after 24 to 48 hours generally.

The dog should be on lead, with a 2-inch-wide leather collar which offers little restriction placed around his neck. We don't want to offer restriction when the dog lashes out. The trainer or pack leader should be at the dog's side.

If the pack leader stands at the animal's side, the dog feels stronger and more secure, for in his anger he will have you, the pack leader, to help in the fight. It is a good idea to start this work in a familiar room which is dark and to stand with your dog backed up to a corner. He will have no place to retreat and so will be inclined to defend himself more vigorously.

The defensive instinct cannot receive impetus or be reinforced by compulsion, nor can the primary inducements which provoke this instinct be given by the trainer. Success depends solely upon the assistants' (criminals) ability to play the part.

The trainer stands at the dog's side. The dog should be standing or in a sitting position. (Never have the dog in the down position at this point.) The

Dowel in hand, the "criminal" moves forward to menace the dog; as soon as the dog advances to repulse his threats, the criminal will beat a hasty retreat. Notice that Lew Burke and the Doberman are backed into a corner of the room to begin with, making retreat on the dog's part impossible. The dog has to make a stand or submit completely; he can't escape.

assistant knocks at the door. He plays with and jiggles the doorknob. He rings the doorbell. He opens the door and enters very slowly and cautiously. He must be afraid because, after all, he doesn't want to get caught by dog, family or police. He hunches over and hesitantly shuffles his feet as he slowly moves against the wall. Suddenly he lunges forward, hoping to arouse the dog; regardless of whether he is successful or not, he immediately moves away with a quick and frightened attitude. Again, he proceeds forward, stepping slowly, hugging the wall, and suddenly he slaps his open palm against the wall and then darts across the room and hugs the opposite wall, always very scared and cautious. He pulls out a six-inch dowel from his back pocket and strikes it at the floor, making challenging but soft sounds at the dog; instantly he backs off and runs away to the opposite wall as if to find a safe place to hide. He slowly shuffles forward, slowly moving his hands in front of him as if to agitate the dog. He continues to move in slowly but very cautiously and frightened. If at any time the dog barks or shows any sign of forward movement, the criminal is to run away and out of the room. The trainer is to try to chase after the criminal with the dog at his side, but he is not to compel the dog to move forward. When the dog stops forward movement, so does the trainer. Great praise is to be given to the dog at this moment. He is to believe he won the fight by chasing the criminal away.

While the assistant is playing his part as criminal, the trainer is to continue to praise the dog and say the word "**Watch**" or any desired word at that time. He is to continue to fondle the dog's head to reassure him. The trainer should have a rhythm such as "Watch him—good puppy." This should continue to be uttered in a soft, syncopated frightened waltz rhythm. The moment the dog shows any sign of aggressiveness or self-protection, the criminal is to run away as the trainer and dog chase him; after the criminal is gone, lavish praise should be given the dog. Repeat the whole operation three or four times and then stop the session. It must be noted that at any time that your dog shows aggression, be it when the assistant first knocks at the door or rings the bell or any time thereafter, praise should be bestowed upon the animal in the most lavish fashion at the very moment of his aggressive demonstration.

The following day have your assistant repeat the provocative action that motivated the dog's defense instinct. Use whatever works and continue to encourage and praise the dog. Our purpose is to create a pleasurable, game-like situation of chase until the dog is conditioned to such a degree that he barks and shows aggression upon merely hearing the phrase "**Watch him**." When response becomes immediate and for real, it is time to move to another and new environment. The dog should not be started on the bite until he is thoroughly conditioned to show aggression on command in all imaginable situations. (Also, his execution of the "out" command, given to make him stop barking, should be perfect. But later for teaching "out.")

If your dog's protective instinct is not sufficiently aroused after two or three weeks of the previously described method, you have no choice other than to offer him a degree of discomfort if he is to become a guard dog. If after the next procedure I describe he doesn't "come out" or offer aggressive behavior, he is simply not the right dog for performing guard work—he's just not cut out for it, so to speak. He is too soft and too docile an animal. A completely trusting and happy animal can become a protection dog. A completely docile one cannot. This is no reason to condemn or reject the animal. Not everyone is capable of being a doctor, a lawyer, a mechanic or whatever, and not every dog is capable of offering protection. If it is necessary to offer discomfort to the dog, the following procedure should be taken: The criminal should repeat the previously described pattern of behavior. (Playing with the doorknob, ringing the doorbell, knocking at the door, entering slowly and cautiously, etc.) However, he should continue with this act until he approaches the dog in his frightened, submissive attitude and if no aggression has been displayed by the animal, the criminal is to grab hold to each of the dog's ears, one in each hand, and then to pull and

This is what you're aiming for: immediate but **controlled** display of aggression at signal from the pack leader. Here Lew Burke has just commanded Buddy, a dog trained by the author to the peak of perfect response, to show his displeasure at an intruder. In other situations, he is a perfectly friendly live-and-let-live animal, as can be seen where he serves as the model for other training situations shown in this book. He is, however, completely dedicated to serving Lew in Lew's position as the true pack leader; regardless of his degree of excitement during attack work, he will cease aggressive or warning behavior immediately upon command from his pack leader. Just as Lew's command to "Watch" is Buddy's signal for adoption of an intense and hostile wariness, Lew's "Out" command is the signal for instantaneous dropping of the attack and resumption of the normal friendly attitude.

twist the ears enough to get a whining reaction, at which point the assistant is to back off with fear radiating from his body. If the dog barks at all, the criminal is to run and the trainer, with the dog at his side, is to pursue. If aggression doesn't occur after several repetitions of ear pulling, stop with the work. Perhaps when the dog gets older he will grow into a less submissive animal and then will be capable. If not, forget it!

No dog should be started on protection work until he is at least a year old. Also, although there are many methods of inflicting pain which can initiate the self-protective instinct in the dog, to the author's way of thinking it is much more sensible to get a dog who has an aptitude for this type of work than to inflict pain upon one who has other qualities. Certainly, ear-pulling is drastic enough.

The reason I approve of ear-pulling and nothing stronger is because some naturally good-humored and loving dogs—the ones that make the best guard dogs—will not bark unless they are hurt once or twice. They are far too trusting and loving of people. These are my favorite types. However, these dogs generally get the idea after having their ears pulled a few times, and the result will be a happy, well adjusted protector. These dogs are not of the overly submissive type. They are great dogs for family and people, and the end result of their training will be well worth the pain that both dog lover and dog feel during the ear-pulling process. That is, of course, if you feel that your dog must offer protection. If not, then just enjoy him and forget the ear-pulling.

Once the dog responds in all situations by barking immediately upon hearing the phrase "watch him," it is time to teach him the meaning of the word "out." "Out" should signify to stop all aggressive behavior immediately. This requires that your

PUTTING ON THE PRONG COL-LAR. Captions on reverse page. See text beginning on page 26.

dog become submissive to you, his pack leader, and it is a very high degree of submissiveness. Therefore, his dependence upon you as his leader becomes magnified. We never start to teach "out" until the dog is very strongly aggressive or protective, for we never want to stifle his protective instinct. Until now, he has won each set-up fight by chasing the criminal beyond out of sight. It must be remembered that at any time that the dog shies away during "Watch Work" the criminal is absolutely never to back the dog up; instead, the criminal is to back away so that the dog can be stimulated afresh. The dog must *never* lose the fight.

After the dog shows confidence and belief in himself (owing to a lack of disagreeable experiences), it is time to expand. At this point, the trainer should tie the dog to a stake secured in the ground. We don't tie him to a fence or anything that he would be tied to in everyday life. We don't want the dog to establish any false or potentially dangerous associations with innocent passersby. The trainer moves away—a distance of about 6 to 10 feet from the dog. Now the animal no longer has the security of the pack leader; he must stand on his own. The agitator should now pretend to be attacking the trainer with several blows and then offer several moves of aggression toward the dog. Then he should return to attacking the pack leader and once again back to the dog. During this time, the trainer should be encouraging the dog by saying "**Watch him—good puppy**" in a continuous waltz rhythm. After a short aggressive display by the dog, the criminal should run off, out of sight and beyond smell. The pack leader should return to the dog and praise him lavishly. The dog has demonstrated real protective qualities, for he has offered aggression when you were attacked as well as himself. Continue with this for about one or two weeks until the dog becomes very strong. You must remember never at any time during "watch work" or protection work to make the dog offer aggression more often than nine to twelve times in one work-out. We don't want him to become bored or overly tired. This is of paramount importance. You can work him twice a day if you like, but never stimulate more than nine to twelve aggressions in one session.

Captions for PUTTING ON THE CHOKE COLLAR. (Photos on reverse page).

Top right: Steven shows the correct way to hold the non-pronged choke collar before putting it onto the dog.

Top left: Putting the collar over the dog's nose.

Bottom left: Continuing over the entire head. If pain or struggle exists because the collar is too tight to slide easily over the dog's ears, get a larger collar.

Bottom right: The collar has been correctly placed around the dog's neck. Notice that to constrict the collar you have to pull downward on the ring. The chain must slide **down** through the other ring, never up. If the collar had been put on incorrectly, one would pull inward to get constriction, thus choking the dog.

PUTTING ON THE CHOKE COLLAR. Captions on reverse page. See text beginning on page 26.

TEACHING TO HEEL. See text beginning on page 30.

Above: the correct initial position. Left: step forward with your left foot as you say "Heel" and simultaneously tap your left side with your palm.

Below right: as the dog pulls ahead, turn about and simultaneously snap the lead; say "Heel" and tap your side. The opposite momentum will offer strong correction. Below left: pat the dog's head and offer praise as the dog performs correctly. (Series continues on page 104.)

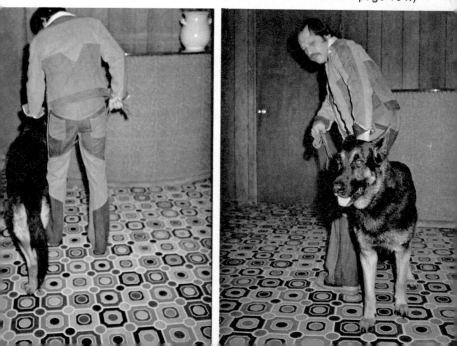

Once the dog seems very confident, you should move farther away from him. Now take a position 15 feet away from the dog and have the assistant repeat his previous behavioral pattern. It is a good idea to use several criminals at this point. If the dog responds only to the original criminal, go back to the lead until the dog responds to everyone. After the dog realizes that each time you are attacked, so is he, he will offer aggression whenever anyone attacks you regardless of how far you are away from him, providing he is able to see the attack. The association of seeing his pack leader being hurt, coupled with the bondage formed as a result of this training, will magnify his sense of comradeship with the pack leader intensely. At this time, the dog can be taught to stop barking at the command "out," or whatever oral signal you want to use as the word association with the cessation of aggression. Always remember to offer praise to the dog whenever he offers aggression when you are attacked, regardless of the distance you are from him.

"OUT"

To have the dog stop showing aggression upon hearing the word "out," the word itself is the primary inducement. The corrections as they are applied are just reinforcing stimuli and compulsions.

Attach a prong collar to the dog's neck so that it is situated above his leather collar. Attach a lead to each collar.

The criminal must stop movement and become completely immobile the instant you command "out." At that very moment you must snap at the lead attached to the prong collar. Snap very gently at first and say "**Out.**" If the dog continues to bark, repeat "**Out**" and snap hard enough to bring him out of his excitement. Immediately praise the dog when he stops barking. The criminal stops moving, thus eliminating the stimulus motivating the dog's chase instinct. You, the pack leader, snap the prong collar, thus inhibiting the dog's aggressive chase. The praise serves as convincing reinforcement. Continue with this until the dog stops showing aggression upon hearing the word "out." Training to the "out" command should require several days of reinforcement.

If the dog stops barking and then starts again, or if he refuses to stop when you snap at the lead, toss the throw chain against his side and simultaneously say "**Out**." This will work. After a short while of conditioning with the chain, if he doesn't immediately respond to the word "out" you will only have to rattle the chain and he will stop barking. You must have some feeling for this type of work. However, you must be certain to have your dog respond to the "out" command immediately with or without the secondary inducement of the rattling of the chain.

MAKING FRIENDS ON COMMAND

After the dog has been called "out" and has stopped showing aggression, command him to sit at your side and fondle his head as you say words of encouragement to him. The criminal does not move. He remains completely immobile exactly at the spot where he was standing when the dog was called out.

The handler allows the lead to remain attached to the prong collar and tells the dog to stay. The handler walks toward the criminal; when he is about two feet away, he says "ok," which to the dog signifies freedom. The dog will run to either the

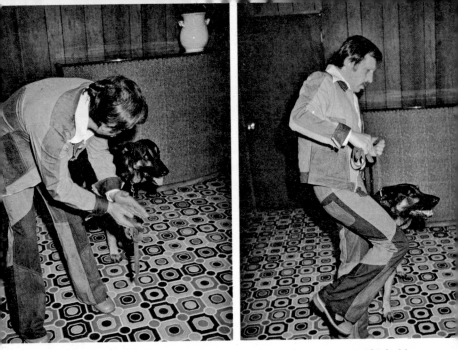

TEACHING TO HEEL continued. (Series begins on page 101.) *Above left:* bending from the waist and clapping hands, thus inducing the dog to catch up and take the desired position. *Above right:* turning left; the dog is too far forward. Bump him with your right knee as you turn left and into him. *Below:* in the photo at left the dog is too far forward and leftward; in the photo at right he's too far behind. In both cases, therefore, the trainer snaps the lead toward the correct direction, hiding his hand from the dog's view as he snaps.

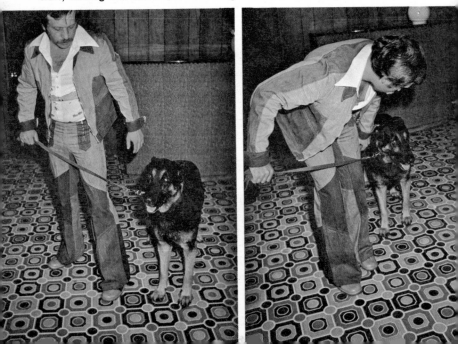

TEACHING THE "SIT." (See text beginning on page 35.) *Above:* the trainer applies pressure to the dog's backside while gently snapping up on the lead. *Below:* the dog has been made to sit.

trainer or the criminal. The trainer is to say "Friends" and repeat this word several times in a high and happy tone.

As the dog approaches the criminal, the trainer is to have his throw chain ready to toss at the dog's side the very moment the dog demonstrates any aggression. The trainer is also to have a switch ready to use if the throw chain is not strong enough. If the dog wags his tail or shows signs of friendliness toward the criminal, praise the animal and repeat the word "friends." The criminal is to remain completely immobile. When there is no movement, 99% of the time the dog will not bite. Even fully trained attack dogs will not bite a man who remains completely still (that is, of course, unless he has been taught to bite a still man). There is no chase. The hunt is over so to speak.

After 20 to 30 seconds the criminal is to say in a high pitched happy tone—"good puppy" and praise the dog. If the animal responds happily, the criminal is to pat the dog's head and praise simultaneously. If the dog doesn't respond in a happy manner, the criminal is to remain still and the trainer is to walk off with the dog. Repeat this exercise until the dog understands that the word "friends" signifies play with the criminal or just detachment from him.

No one will get hurt if the criminal does not move. Also, the trainer must have the chain and switch ready to use if necessary. The more friendly and less suspicious a dog is, the better he will eventually make "friends." Dogs who hold a grudge or who are timid are not particularly suitable for learning to make friends.

It should be noted that the dog while being taught to "watch" should not be made to bark for more than one minute at a time. We don't want to make him tired.

ATTACK ON LEAD—
Criminal Wears Suit and/or Arm Protector or Sleeve

The criminal stands perfectly visible, in a peaceful attitude, motionless, his arms hanging loosely and holding in his right hand a stick two feet long and about ¾ of an inch wide, hidden against his leg and pointing downwards.

The trainer holds the dog close to him to offer security, but the lead is a long one. He walks toward the criminal, with the dog at his left side. His manner of approach should be casual. The criminal should be engaged in conversation by the trainer for a few minutes. Suddenly, without warning to the dog, the criminal should assume a hostile attitude. He smacks the stick against the ground near the dog and retreats as he does so. He talks angrily at the dog as he backs away and smacks the stick against his sleeve or protective suit. If the dog doesn't pursue, he strikes the stick lightly against the dog's forelegs and retreats with head down, as a scared criminal would back off. During this time the trainer holds the lead short while saying **"Fass"** or any word chosen to eventually mean attack. If the dog moves forward, encourage him. If he hesitates, move up with the dog to encourage him. The animal must never, however, be given the opportunity to grab hold of the stick. Also, he must never be backed off. The dog must always think he is the winner. At the moment the dog moves forward, the criminal is to run off, holding his stick high, and the trainer is to run alongside of the dog with shouts of encouragement like **"Good puppy. Good dog."** The criminal is then to find a car to hide behind. Make certain to use only the leather collar when doing this type of work. We don't want to restrain the dog.

TEACHING THE "SIT-STAY." (See text beginning on page 38.) Keeping the dog in position by maintaining the open hand in front of him (upper photos), Robert Burke moves (bottom left) as far away as the lead will allow. At bottom right he snaps up on the lead, correcting the dog as he is about to move forward and therefore compelling him to stay.

TEACHING THE "DOWN" COMMAND. (See text beginning on page 41.) With the dog in the sitting position (lower photo) Mrs. Ann Burke extends her right arm over her head while keeping the lead between the heel and sole of her shoe. The lead will therefore slide easily while she pulls up on it and gives the command "Down." In the upper photo, the dog is down in an attitude of complete submission.

After a few minutes of rest, repeat the above exercise. As soon as the dog charges, chase after the fleeing criminal, again praising the animal in the process. Repeat this six to nine times, then stop. Remember—most importantly, the dog must never be backed off. Therefore, whenever the criminal strikes the stick anywhere, he must retreat slowly and cautiously. When the dog finally charges—the criminal runs off and hides. At the end of each chase, the trainer praises the dog and dog-plays with him as a pack member.

If during the chase the dog stops, the criminal should immediately turn about and again swing his stick and tease the dog. When the animal offers forward movement, the criminal is to run off. But remember that we never want to tire the dog, so six to nine repetitions is plenty.

Repeat this procedure for several days until the dog seems eager to chase and to capture or bite. At this point, the criminal should now not wear his protective sleeve. Instead, he should hold a bunched-up potato sack made of light webbing in his left hand and a stick in his right hand. Again, he is to stand about 10 or 15 feet away from the dog and trainer, with the dog at the trainer's left side. The trainer says "**Fass**," and the criminal instantly smacks the stick against the ground to the right and left of the dog and now moves in one step and away again. The trainer holds the dog tightly and in a frightened voice commands "**Fass**." At the exact moment the dog seems to be outraged, as though he might bite, the trainer is to repeat "fass" and the criminal is to offer the sack. When the dog takes hold of it, the criminal is to move the sack up and down offering a tug of war, inspiring the dog to pull harder. After several seconds the criminal is to let go of the sack and run off and hide. The trainer runs with the dog

The dog vents his fury on the sack as the criminal prepares to flee.

TEACHING THE "DOWN-STAY." (See text beginning on page 43.) *Above:* Eleven-year-old Stacey Burke is telling Buddy to "Stay" as she extends her open left palm in front of his face. *Below right:* Stacey is at a distance from Buddy. She says "Stay" and keeps her open palm extended. The lead is held without slack, thus further inducing the stay. *Below left:* Stacey is at the end of the 6-foot lead. Notice that her open palm is still extended toward Buddy and the lead is held without slack.

TEACHING TO SIT FROM THE DOWN POSITION. See text beginning on page 44.

Stacey is saying "Sit" to the Springer Spaniel as she walks in toward the dog and gently pulls up on the lead.

Since the dog was not sitting by the time she reached him, she is applying very mild pressure upon his paws.

The dog is now in the desired sitting position.

Stacey is verbally and physically praising the Springer Spaniel after he sits.

in pursuit and continues to shout words of praise and encouragement. After trainer and dog return to their original spot, dog pack play should take place for several seconds. The dog should be made to feel the happiness of the pack leader. Repeat this exercise six to nine times. Each time the criminal is to feed the sack lightly and offer the tug of war resistance for several seconds and then run off. The dog must always emerge victorious. He and the pack leader pursue together while chasing after the criminal. Repeat this for several days until merely upon the word "fass" and the sight of the criminal with sack in hand, the dog is excited and wants to bite. At this point, the sack is no longer used. The criminal now repeats the same exercise using a sleeve.

We started with the sack because it was much easier and less distasteful to take hold of than the sleeve, which is thicker and more difficult to grasp. Therefore, conditioning on the sack should be very strong before moving on to the use of the sleeve.

Again, the criminal follows the same procedure. At the height of excitement, the trainer says "Fass" and the criminal feeds the sleeve. When the dog takes hold, the criminal offers a brief fight by moving the sleeve up and down and to him and away, but never too strongly for the dog to handle, because we don't want to create a losing situation for the animal. Then the criminal assistant should run off and hide, leaving the dog biting the sleeve. Once again the trainer and dog should chase after him, thus encouraging the dog to leave the sleeve and get the man. After several repetitions, stop.

Continue with this procedure for several days until the dog bites hard at the sleeve and continues to bite hard. If the dog ever releases the bite before the criminal takes flight, the criminal is to poke the stick at the dog's side or offer some antagonizing gesture to reinstate excitement and anger in the animal. During the first several days, the dog should not be made to fight or bite the sleeve for more than 5 to 15 seconds. Remember, the dog must always emerge a confident winner and never be made to feel overtired or bored or to lose confidence.

When the time comes that the dog is very positively animated in his forward attack and in his taking hold of the sleeve and in fighting with the criminal, at this point the criminal is to use the stick to poke the dog's side. This will increase the dog's anger and will motivate him to fight harder, thereby creating a greater degree of courage, for at the end the dog will win as he chases the criminal away.

After reaching the point at which the dog immediately attacks upon command, you should employ a new assistant. Also, at this point, you should change locations each day. The dog must not associate one criminal and one environment with this sort of play.

Assistants should be changed regularly now, as should locations, until the dog automatically responds to the command "fass." As the training proceeds, the duration of the fight (tug of war) with the sleeve can be made longer—but never to the point of the dog's exhaustion. Also, the use of the stick is no longer necessary. The assistant can use a starter's pistol. Before each attack, the criminal is to shoot off the gun. The trainer immediately says "**Fass**." Teasing continues and the dog bites. The assistant can use a knife or change to any and all instruments you wish to condition the dog to regard as dangerous. It's just a matter of conditioning through association. After this has been accomplished, it is time to teach the dog to respond to the word "out," or to stop biting.

BREAKING THE DOG FROM JUMPING ONTO PEOPLE.

A German Shepherd is jumping onto twelve-year-old Elizabeth Burke.

Elizabeth places her knee in the Shepherd's stomach. He never saw anything, but he feels discomfort when up on Elizabeth.

TEACHING TO GO TO HEEL. See text beginning on page 49.

Stepping backwards with right foot and gently snapping the lead, thus inducing the dog to chase after your retreating leg.

Left: the dog's head has gone past the trainer's retreated right leg. *Right:* the lead has been transferred from the trainer's right hand to his left. He is stepping forward with his left leg. (Series continues on page 120.)

A prong collar in addition to the leather one is placed around the dog's neck. A lead is attached to each collar. The dog is put on the attack and after a brief fight, the trainer commands in a strong, loud voice "**Out**" and simultaneously snaps hard at the prong collar as the criminal freezes but does not let go of the sleeve. If the dog doesn't leave the bite, the trainer is to repeat "out" and simultaneously toss the throw chain at the dog's side as he again snaps the lead. At the moment the dog leaves the bite, the trainer is to offer lavish praise as the criminal remains perfectly motionless. Repeat this several times for as many days as is necessary for the dog to leave the bite merely upon the word "out" and without use of the chain. Remember, the trainer is never to allow himself to be in front of the dog, for he may get bitten owing to the excitement of the animal.

After the dog has sufficiently been conditioned to attack on lead and to leave the bite at hearing the word "out" without use of the chain, you may move on to off-the-lead attack. During work on "out," the criminal must be certain to offer no movement, so the dog will have nothing to fight or pull against.

OFF-LEAD ATTACK

Start off-lead attack training by having the assistant tease the animal from a distance of about 15 to 20 feet away. The dog is wearing only the leather collar attached to a 6-foot lead which you can unsnap or unhook easily. The criminal is wearing a sleeve, and as he agitates uses his hand to bang at one spot on his sleeve. When the dog is in a state of excited rage, unhook the lead and simultaneously say "**Fass**." The criminal is to move backward as the dog chases after him. The criminal feeds the sleeve and the dog bites. The trainer is to shout

If the dog has been raised to the proper pitch of frenzy by the agitations of the criminal he will attack the sleeve as soon as he's released from the lead.

GO TO HEEL continued from page 117.

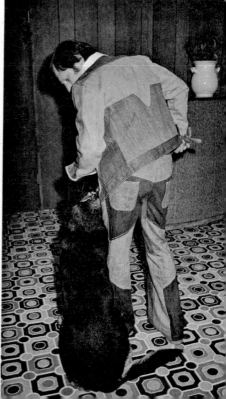

Opposite: *Top left:* the dog is now passing behind the trainer. He is not pursuing forward body movements, so the trainer gently snaps the lead in the desired direction. *Top right:* the dog approaches the trainer's left side. The trainer bends at the waist, encouraging the dog to come to his side. *Bottom left:* the trainer leans his left hip into the dog, inducing him to sit. *Bottom right:* the dog is sitting at the trainer's left side and being praised.

Above: a mixed-breed dog attached to a stall chain in hopes of preventing excretion. *Below:* a Chow Chow penned in a cage as an excretion-preventing technique.

words of encouragement—"**Good puppy**." After 5 to 15 seconds of biting, the trainer commands "Out." The criminal freezes but always keeps the sleeve in front of him to make certain to protect himself. If the dog doesn't leave the bite upon hearing the word "out," the trainer is to throw the chain hard at the side of the dog. The moment the dog ceases to bite, the trainer is to offer lavish praise and affection. Then command the dog to "heel" and walk off with him. The criminal is not to move. Repeat this six to nine times a day for as many days as is necessary to make the dog respond to "fass" and "out" instantly upon command.

After the conditioning has been perfected, you may employ other criminals to play various roles. Each may use a starter pistol, knife or whatever you wish for the dog to associate with danger and "fass." If the dog knows that each time he hears a gun shot, he sees the gun and the criminal and he attacks, he will soon learn that the gun is dangerous.

Some dogs will leave the bite more quickly than others. In order to attain instant results, a slingshot propelled marble that strikes the dog's side simultaneously with his hearing the word "out" will insure 100% and instant response.

This work is very serious and can be dangerous if not done correctly. No dog should kill a person. If the criminal is not capable of offering any more danger or fight, the dog should be conditioned to stop biting *instantly* upon hearing the pack leader's command "out." Therefore, use the slingshot if necessary. If you are not capable, employ a qualified trainer to do so. One or two well aimed shots should do the trick.

Continue off-lead attack training until the dog will chase after the criminal and bite from any reasonable distance. This will be accomplished by

Here Buddy is making an instantaneous response to Lew Burke's "out" call. For the safety of the criminal, it is absolutely imperative that the dog's response to the "out" command be unquestioned.

having the assistant move farther back 10 to 20 feet at a time after each day of successful work. Remember, never release the dog from the lead until he is in a frenzy. After this has been accomplished, it is time to work with no lead at all. From a down-stay position, with you standing at the dog's side, command "Fass." The criminal is to run away, offering the dog a chase. As the dog approaches, the criminal is to stand hard, bracing himself to withstand the dog's impact. The criminal does not want to fall down, for this will increase danger to him. When the dog hits, a tug of war fight pursues. The trainer runs forward and when upon the scene he says "Out" and enforces the command. Immediately lavish praise follows. After several days of this exercise we move on.

Above left: giving the suppository. The trainer strokes the dog's loins and gently says, "Good puppy," thus putting the dog at ease. He gently puts the suppository into the rectum a little at a time and very gently continues to re-assure the animal with praise. He always tries to make it a pleasurable experience so that the dog will not panic. However, if the dog should panic, tie him to a stall chain and give the suppository by standing at the end of the extended chain. By doing this, he cannot bite you when he panics. Remember to be gentle and generally you won't have a problem. *Above right:* the dog starting to defecate. *Below:* the fecal matter has been expelled, and the trainer then is lavish with verbal praise.

TEACHING TO COME. (See text beginning on page 53.) The trainer steps back, thus inducing the dog to chase or come; simultaneously, she snaps the lead and says "Come," while snapping her fingers. (Photo series continues on page 128.)

Now it is time to have the dog attack without command. The dog is made to lie down and to stay. The trainer walks off, joining the criminal, who is about 20 feet away.

After several seconds, the criminal suddenly pretends to attack the trainer. He swings the stick at him, he shouts, he may fire the starter's pistol. The trainer backs away as if being beaten. As he does so, he commands "**Fass.**"

Upon responding to the "fass" command under these circumstances, the dog is to receive most lavish praise; he is no longer protecting only himself. He, the dog, could just as easily have turned away and run off to save himself. Instead, he has come to help you, and the praise should be given accordingly. Continue with this for several days until the dog automatically, and instantly, without any command, comes out and attacks the criminal merely upon seeing you being attacked. No verbal command should be necessary to inspire this behavior. Only the command "out" is needed, and that only to stop the attack.

Start each day's work with one or two on-lead bites, then two or three off-lead bites. End each session with the criminal attacking you from a distance. At this point we move on to teaching the dog to bite a man not wearing protective clothing. To accomplish this, start by going back to holding the dog at your left side and on the lead. The familiar criminal appears about 10 feet away. He is wearing ordinary street clothes. Once again, he has a stick hidden at his side. Also, he has protective gear beneath his street clothes so that he doesn't get hurt. Command "**Watch.**" At this moment, the assistant agitates by striking the ground and teasing the dog. When the dog is extremely excited, unfasten the lead and say "**Fass.**"

With the stick hidden behind him at his side, the criminal approaches; he appears to be dressed in ordinary street clothes, but of course he is wearing protective clothing.

The criminal should move back and offer his arm. The moment the dog takes hold, praise him. After a few seconds, call him "out." If the dog doesn't bite, the criminal must poke the stick at the dog's side to infuriate him, but he is never to hurt the dog to the point of discouragement. If the dog doesn't bite, more conditioning on the sleeve is necessary. Continue with this biting a man wearing street clothes as you did with previously described exercises.

One can teach the dog to stop biting immediately after the man stops offering flight or resistance. This is accomplished merely by enforcing the

TEACHING TO COME. (Photo series continued from page 125.) *Upper photos:* the Puli (shown sitting in photo at right) has reacted to the inducement and (photo left) is standing and moving toward the trainer. *Lower photos:* at left the dog has come to the trainer. As the dog approached, she took one step into him and gently snapped up on the lead, compelling him to sit in front of her. At right the dog is rewarded through patting and verbal praise.

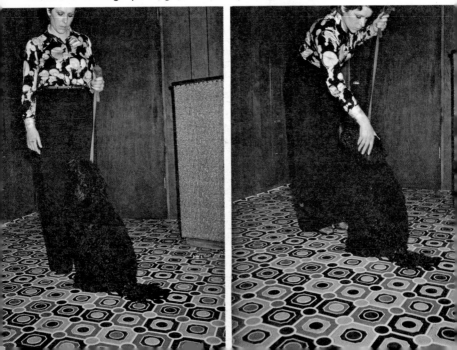

BARK ON COMMAND. (See text beginning on page 91.) *Left:* Doberman Pinscher on a stall chain before training session begins. Notice the leather collar adjacent to the prong collar.

Top right: the assistant enters in a frightened manner after having banged on the door, played with the knob, and rung the bell. He is hugging the wall in simulated fright. *Below left:* he continues to act frightened as he shuffles forward. *Below right:* he lunges forward to arouse the dog. (Series continues on page 132.)

command "out" at desired moments and to maintain this pattern of conditioning throughout.

In police-type work, it is very often desired that the dog pursue the criminal and, upon reaching him, not bite but merely bark and hold him at bay. This can be accomplished by changing our initial procedure. From the start, when the dog offers strong aggression on the command "watch," the criminal is to use the stick. Whenever the dog comes within reach, the assistant is to strike the side of the dog's face with the stick hard enough to make him stick-shy but not hard enough to discourage him completely. On each occasion, the trainer is to snap the long lead back. If this is continued throughout, the dog will soon come to know that he must circle and evade possible blows until the arrival of the police officer. This same dog can be taught to bite, but never when the officer is not present. He will bite only on command or when the officer is being attacked.

One should never teach a dog to be stick-shy if you want him for home or commercial purposes. If a criminal is wielding a gun, the dog should hit instantly. The sight of a raging animal will very often cause misfire and panic on the part of the criminal. But if the dog stands off, he has no chance. He is a sitting duck. He must hit the gunman instantly. Therefore, for home or most commercial uses, we don't want to make the dog stick-shy. He should be conditioned to hit upon sighting a weapon. However, for home use, gun and weapon conditioning should not be done. For one thing, children play with toy weapons, and a dog who has been conditioned to respond to weapons presents a danger in such situations. Consequently, weapon training should be carried out only if the dog will be used in appropriate environments.

HOLD AT BAY

Once the dog has mastered hitting on and off the lead, we move on to "hold at bay." After being called "out," the dog should instantly leave the bite. At this point, the pack leader calls "**Come**." The dog must immediately return to the leader. The master now commands "**Down**" and then "**Stay**." Therefore, the off-lead obedience must be flawless. Now, the criminal must remain motionless. The trainer walks to the criminal. The criminal attacks the pack leader. The dog automatically attacks the criminal. After several repetitions, using the same procedure, the master now walks away; he should go out of the dog's sight but be in a strategic area where he, the master, can easily observe both dog and criminal. The dog is 10 feet away from the criminal. If the dog leaves the down-stay position, the master immediately reappears and reinforces down and stay. Again, the master hides. Now, the criminal suddenly and without warning bangs his stick against the ground and agitates until the dog attacks. After a few moments, the criminal stops all movement. The dog should leave the bite and just observe, waiting for more action. If he doesn't stop biting, the master reappears and enforces "out." Continue with this exercise until the dog instantly hits the criminal upon the slightest movement and stops biting when the criminal becomes motionless. The use of a throw chain or, as a last resort, the slingshot, will insure instant release upon immobility.

MAKING FRIENDS

This procedure is the same as was previously described with the "watch" command. After the dog has been called "out," the trainer must say

BARK ON COMMAND. (Series continued from page 129.) *Top:* the dog is backed up into a corner. He has no place to retreat to. The trainer has the dog at his left side and holds the lead with his left arm extended straight out so that he is able to keep the dog from biting him if the animal should ever turn to bite the closest thing to him while in a state of passionate fury. Notice that the trainer's face is not in front of the dog. *Bottom:* the dog is aroused very strongly.

The assistant
ntinues to agitate;
ow he has a dowel.
e criminal will poke
t the dog's head in
all directions to
gitate him and will
ickly pull his hand
k to encourage the
chase instinct.

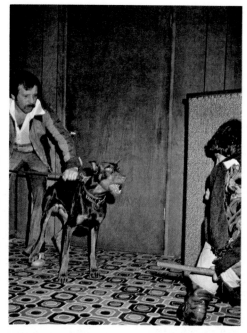

Left: pulling and twisting the dog's ears as a last resort to evoke aggressive response. Notice that the criminal's arms are parallel; if he holds onto the ears the dog will not be able to bite him. When the assistant lets go, he must instantly run away. Below: the assistant strikes the short dowel against the floor.

"**Okay**," suggesting freedom; then say "**Friends**." The criminal remains frozen as the master and dog play. When the dog sniffs and inspects the criminal, the trainer is to repeat "ok" and "friends." If the dog's attitude is stand-offish, the criminal is to remain completely immobile. If the dog offers friendliness, the criminal is to offer friendship and play. During this exercise, the trainer is to be completely on top of the situation. Included in this exercise, the trainer and criminal should sit next to one another talking peacefully and having fun. The criminal never pays attention to the dog unless the animal approaches him. At this time, the criminal offers only kind words—never fast or jerky movements. The trainer is always to observe so that he is ready to stop the dog if necessary. After many repetitions of seeing the trainer talking and getting along with the criminal, the dog will come to understand that this is most acceptable, and that there is no reason to offer aggression unless the criminal suddenly were to become an assailant.

Teaching Food Refusal

The reasons for teaching food refusal vary. Our purpose in teaching the dog never to take food except from his own pack members is solely to save the dog's life through conditioning, thereby preventing him from eating poisonous foods.

Eating is a natural drive in all dogs. They must eat to stay alive. Naturally, eating is a most pleasurable experience. This pleasurable memory must become highly displeasurable in all situations and environments where his own pack members are not the ones directly offering the food. Therefore, the conditioning process must be painful to dog lover and dog, and it must occur each time the dog shows even the slightest interest in food at any time the trainer is not the direct provider.

Step I—The dog is on the lead sitting at his trainer's left. A stranger approaches in a very friendly manner. When in front of the dog, the stranger squats (deep knee bend) and offers food in his open palm. The instant the dog shows intention of eating, the stranger is to come across with his other hand and slap the side of the dog's face very hard. Then, the stranger is to run off. This must be repeated until the dog either refuses to eat from the stranger's hand or offers the stranger aggression.

Step II—The trainer is to take walks with the dog. Various types of foods are to be strategically placed prior to the walk. Whenever the dog shows interest in any of the food, the trainer is to instantly say "**No,**" and simultaneously toss the throw chain at the dog's side. This should be done in new and strange environments as well as familiar ones.

Step III—The dog is set free in his yard area. The trainer is hiding. The dog must not see the

WATCH WORK. (See text beginning on page 96.) The assistant offers aggression to both the trainer and the dog. The trainer says "Watch him" and "Good puppy." In the upper photo, notice the assistant's right arm ready to strike out in the direction of the dog. Here a park bench is used as the site for attachment of the lead, but normally a stake should be used.

ATTACK ON LEAD. (See text beginning on page 107.) *Above:* the trainer says "Fass." The dog is held on the lead as he attacks the sack that the criminal offers to his mouth. *Below:* the dog has taken hold of the sack, and now the criminal moves it up and down, offering a tug of war and inspiring the dog to pursue. The criminal is about to let go of the sack and run off.

trainer, but the trainer must have complete view of the animal. A stranger approaches and tosses food over the fence. The moment the dog demonstrates interest in the food, the trainer is to instantly employ one of the standard dissuaders discussed earlier, with slingshot and marble the dissuader of last resort. This must be repeated until the dog shows no interest at all in foods thrown over the fence.

Step IV—This is a variation of the above to cover training the dog not to eat foods that he discovers in his travels, whether on your property or elsewhere, whereas *Step III* describes the process of training the dog not to eat foods presented to him by unseen forces. Prior to letting the dog run free and supposedly unsupervised in the yard, have an assistant scatter foods in various locations. Again the trainer is to be hidden from the dog. The moment the dog demonstrates any interest in any of the foods, the trainer is to use the slingshot and shoot the dog with a marble. Within a relatively short period of time, the dog will come to associate displeasure with the sight of foods when not offered directly by a pack member.

How To Read A Dog

This chapter is meant to help all those who are aspiring dog trainers. Some dog owners pay top dollar to people who profess to be trainers but in reality have little knowledge or talent. Some have been professing to be trainers for many years. Please don't misunderstand. My intention is not negative or intended to demean anyone—it is intended to assist you in reading and understanding a strange dog. Your comprehension of training literature, coordinated with your craftmanship, determines your success when training any dog. Therefore, this chapter will help all dog owners to better understand dogs and be able to train their own better.

When a dog comes to a trainer's kennel, he suffers greatly, for his pack leader is gone. Regardless of how weak or inadequate his leader may have been, he is missed. It will generally require approximately 18 hours for the dog to come around and be ready to accept new and temporary leadership. During this period of time you ought not to push yourself upon him.

If he is a friendly dog, offer friendship and all that goes along with friendship. However, if he is mistrusting (which commonly means that he is aggressive), your approach should be very calculated.

Dogs demonstrate aggressive behavior for various reasons. Some are shy and react aggressively only in an attempt to scare everyone away (so that they will be left alone). They are saying—"please keep away," as they bark and show their teeth. The showing of teeth could be taken as the rough equivalent to one man's telling another about his fighting prowess so that he himself is not put to the test.

I must digress briefly at this point. It is my view that no man wants to fight. If he says he does, he is a

ATTACK ON LEAD. (See text beginning on page 114.) *Above:* the dog hits the sleeve. *Below:* the criminal rotates the sleeve in a tug of war.

ATTACK ON LEAD. (See text beginning on page 115.) *Above:* the dog is aware of the oncoming man. *Below:* the dog has been told to watch as the criminal begins his menacing gestures with the weapon. (Series continues on page 144.)

liar. Man fights or pretends to be tough because of his own personal hangups, but in reality he shakes like a leaf in the wind before every fight. If he doesn't shake, he can't fight, or he never had one! I know this to be fact. During my life, I have had at least 1,000 street fights, 22 amateur boxing matches and 10 professional fights and I must tell you, I can fight! I was overly respected for this talent as a youngster in both the street and the ring—and I shook like a leaf before every fight I ever had! If not externally, certainly internally. The same is true with all good fighters, and bad ones for that matter. I know, because they have told me so in complete honesty, and I know because I lived it! The dog is no different in this respect.

One of the basic natural drives present in all animals is to stay alive. If in doubt, the most coura-geous will cop out—unless the mind is blurred at the moment. Bewilderment combined with sudden fright results in confused fantasy. Consequently, at a given moment, any man is capable of killing—even the so-called most well adjusted. The same is true with any animal who is adequately equipped to kill another. I am certain that I am able to expound on this point endlessly so that even the most protec-tive will agree—but that is another book perhaps. The dog is no different from man in this respect. Man has his God. The dog has his pack leader. In the absence of security, many men and many dogs fall apart. This is perhaps one of the reasons why most dogs have liked man since their first association.

When a new dog comes into your kennel, he is filled with insecurity. Avoiding the fight is most beneficial for all concerned. If you beat him out of his aggression you will defeat him, but you won't gain his trust or confidence. Your job is to give the animal confidence and security. This can be achieved only through careful handling. You must never push him into a corner. He must never feel that he *has* to fight. It is far better to employ psychology from the start so that no conditioned mistrust is connected with you. The mistrust and aggression he offers at the start are a result of his previous life. He associates you with his past. As his educator, you have responsibility for gaining his friendship and trust. If not, you can't educate him. You can only beat him. The results are obvious to all—thank God!

With the aggressive dog, you must first read his kind of aggression. Most—but not all—aggressive dogs that I have met are shy. Let us first consider the shy dog, remembering that our aim is to make friends with the dog before starting to teach him.

MAKING FRIENDS WITH SHY DOGS

There are four degrees of shy dogs according to my categorization. They are:

(A) *Degree I Shy Dog*—This dog is somewhat stand-offish. He will bark at you only if you back away in complete fright. Generally, he will look at you with his tail at approximately a 45° downward angle to the rectum. His bark will have some hoarseness to it, but it will be short barks with every so often a higher octave blending within each bark. He will not bite unless your non-talent to provoke this quality is exceptional. Only extreme teasing or evidence of fright on your part will make him bite. You as the pack leader must remember never to show fright to any animal, because your fright will cause him to mistrust you. It is all right for your "criminal" assistant to show fright during guard training, but you, the pack leader, must never show fright. If I were introduced to you and upon introduction I pulled my hand away and stepped back-

ATTACK ON LEAD. (Series continued from page 141.)
Upper photo: the dog offers the ultimate in open-mouthed, bare-fanged aggression as the criminal advances and menaces with the weapon. *Lower photo:* Lew Burke's wonder dog, Buddy, the dog in all of the attack sequences, is so automatic in his responses that at this point the command "Out" has already caused him to lose all desire to continue his aggressive behavior.

OFF-LEAD ATTACK. (See text beginning on page 118.) The trainer stands next to the criminal, about 20 feet away from the dog, who maintains a vigilant but unaggressive posture. (Series continues on page 148.)

wards, you wouldn't trust me. The dog will demonstrate his mistrust through barking and body movement.

(B) *Degree II Shy Dog*—This dog will demonstrate his feelings, temperament and disposition by keeping his tail at approximately a 10° angle to the rectum. It will be almost between his legs. He is more stand-offish; as he backs away, he will be clacking his teeth. His barks are of a higher pitch than the first type, and his teeth are far more visible. At times, his barking will be as deep-throated as that of the Degree I shy dog, but his stand-offishness is much more apparent. As you move in, he backs off, and as you back off he instantly charges with full voice, seemingly wanting to tear you apart. If you would strike him two times with a switch across the side of the face, he would hide in his corner. If you approach him brazenly, he will back off and be completely submissive. But if at any moment after you approach you shy away for even one second, he will bite you. This is the dog most responsible for biting people without due cause.

You must remember that upon completion of training, you must instruct the owner of a dog of this type that when he walks this dog at the heel position, he should always keep a big slack in the lead. If the lead is held tightly by the pack leader, even the best trained Degree II shy dog will strain to bite a passerby. The tight lead suggests to this type of dog that there is something to mistrust. Also, he feels his master at the other end of the lead, which connotes to him the feeling that the pack leader will support him in the fight, thus giving him false confidence. When walking this type of dog, the pack leader must always keep slack in the lead. This type of dog will generally respond sharply and quickly to commands. He will be most accurate. This is due to his personality. However, he should always be supervised when strangers are present.

(C) *Degree III Shy Dog*—This type of dog is in a frenzy. He will run away upon seeing a stranger and will hide in a corner. If the stranger takes one backward step, he will usually pursue while barking most aggressively and showing plenty of teeth. If the stranger were suddenly to stop short, the dog would immediately retreat to a corner and stop barking. His barking is in a still higher voice. He only wants to be left alone. If you walk by him and ignore him, he won't utter a sound. But if you walk by him and slowly back away, he will respond instantly by moving forward at almost the same velocity as you use in backing off (he won't take a chance by moving in faster than you back away).

While lying in his corner, this dog generally holds his tail between and under his legs. As you back off and trigger his aggression, he will generally bark in a high-pitched yet hoarse voice, and the tail will be close to or remain between his legs.

Some dogs of this type, however, will not bark at all. They will only remain in their corner as you back away. They will show aggression only if you approach them directly, head on so to speak, and then suddenly back away. They are extremely frightened and will sometimes urinate while lying in the corner if your approach is too sudden or too threatening. These dogs can be trained; they can be excellent pets in the proper environment. They will bark at the door when strangers arrive. They will put up a good front to the scared or ignorant, for they will demonstrate all teeth. Generally, they are very easy to handle within the home, their most secure place of existence. They do very well in the

OFF-LEAD ATTACK. (Series continued from page 145.) *Above:* the trainer and criminal face each other at a distance prior to the attack. *Below:* the trainer has commanded the dog to attack, and the criminal has braced himself for the hit.

The trainer has approached to call the dog "Out." Because of the aggressive fury aroused in the dog by attack training at this level, the safety of the person playing the role of the criminal demands that the dog have been trained to immediate response to the "Out" command.

home of people who never before owned a dog, as well as with weak pack leaders.

Degree IV Shy Dog—This dog is the one I assume to be like a fox. He would stay in his corner and bark in a high screaming voice at anyone who comes across his path. He never moves forward. His only desire is to be away from people. If people approach and back off suddenly, he still remains in his corner. If he steps out, it is a body movement only. If he barks, he will spit as he does so.

Many so-called dog people suggest putting a dog to sleep for various reasons. They feel that this type of dog especially should be "put down." My feelings are that we have no right to pass such judgment. We have no right to take life. I most honestly feel that there is a place for every dog and that we mortals have no justification in assuming such power.

This Degree IV shy dog is almost non-existent as far as my experiences have provided. One's responsibility is to find some situation under which this dog can live free from his fears. . . perhaps a yard situation in which he has the protection and support of other dogs in a pack. He may well trust other dogs, for he understands them far better than he does people.

As certain breeds burgeon in popularity, unscrupulous breeders who care more about making money than they do about the breed will mate one genetically disturbed animal to another. The pups will be sold and in many cases eventually will reproduce. This practice should be strictly curbed.

As was mentioned earlier in the book, there are three types of shy dogs: the genetically shy dog, the man-made shy dog and the environmentally shy dog. Each can be helped considerably through good obedience training. However, the genetically shy dog will be helped in gaining of confidence to a lesser degree than the other two types.

The methods of approaching the shy dog really depend on the situation. If the owner of the dog is present, have him quickly slip the lead into your hand; as soon as you get the lead, walk off with the dog. Once his master is no longer present and you are controlling him with the lead, you will have succeeded in showing the dog that in the absence of his pack leader (and thus the absence of his security blanket) he is being controlled; this gives you the temporary leadership role and also shows the dog that he is not being harmed. If he should attempt to bite you, don't hit him. Hitting will only increase his fear. If he tries to bite, simply hold him off with the lead by extending and stiffening your arm, thus keeping the dog's mouth out of reach of your body. When putting this dog on a stall chain or into a cage, it is a good practice to leave the lead attached to his collar. If you do this, it will be much easier for you to handle him the next time you approach. All you will have to do is to grab hold of the lead, which will communicate to the dog control and leadership. Also, you will easily be able to prevent him from biting.

When approaching the shy dog who has been tied to the stall chain or who is in a cage, never move in on him by standing up. Your aim should be to make him feel as unthreatened as possible. You should assume a deep knee bend position, arms extended in front of you and parallel to the ground, and beneath his chest if possible. You should duck walk toward him, slowly inching your way in and constantly saying in a high-pitched caressing voice "**Good puppy**." You want to get the dog to forget about his fear. By assuming this posture, you are coming down to his size and will seem like less of a threat. Once you are within reach of the lead, quickly and without hesitation take hold of it. Continue to talk to him. Soon after, take him for a walk. After a

Top left: the undersleeve worn by the criminal to protect himself when he is not wearing the heavily padded outside sleeve (shown above). The coat he puts on will hide the undersleeve. Lower photos on this page and upper photos on opposite page show the ravaging the coat takes from the dog.

Above: illustrating why a coat can quickly get ripped during training sessions. The dog is tenacious and has sharp teeth.

Below: the attack dog is shown making friends with the criminal. He is not paying any attention to the sleeve, thus illustrating that when he attacks it is not necessarily the sleeve he is after. The erstwhile criminal, the complete center of the dog's savage fury only moments before these photos were taken, is now regarded as a friend and allowed to pat him.

short while, he will have more trust, as he will see that he has not been harmed. When this takes place, offer the back of your hand to his mouth. If he shies away, don't force yourself on him; merely praise him, trying to reassure the animal, and continue walking. After several attempts and as the walking continues, he will come to trust you more. Your aim is to enter into dog pack play with him, with you as a dog companion. You must take as much time as necessary to gain his confidence and trust before assuming the pack leader role and before starting to train him.

THE BOLD BITER, OR HIGHLY AGGRESSIVE DOG

Any dog can be taught not to bite. This has been indicated previously when teaching the command "no" and when working on the dog-fighting problem. If each time the dog attempts to bite he instantly receives painful corrections such as the switch or slingshot, or even a quick well placed strike across the bridge of his nose with a dowel, biting will cease. Also, later obedience lessons he learns will play a part in maintaining control over this problem, after the primary conditioning has been completed.

The biting problem generally is not completely eliminated in the way that a surgeon would cut away a foreign body. The problem is generally only arrested. The dog has come to associate displeasure and pain with each attempt to bite. To avoid the pain which he recalls most vividly, he no longer bites. If his pack leader is strong in nature, he is a lucky dog, because this type of dog requires a man who will demand strict and exact obedience and enforce each command to the fullest. If this dog does not believe that his master is his genuine pack leader, he will eventually regress to his former behavior pattern. This dog also is prone to regression in the absence of the pack leader. The master must be schooled well as to how to be the dog's true leader. Thus, when the dog tests the master (challenges him for pack leadership), and he will, the master will be able to establish himself firmly.

The biting problem generally begins when the dog is a puppy. He will bark at strangers. Each time the barking occurs and the stranger backs off or shies away, the dog believes he has won the fight. Eventually, he will have won so many barking bouts that he will start to believe in himself just as the neighborhood bully would. And so, eventually, after enough confidence has been gained, he will pursue the fight further and will bite. The more fights he wins, the more confident and convinced he becomes. I have seen dogs of this type who have eventually come to challenge their family pack members. At some point during the development or after the formation of this behavioral pattern, the trainer is called. In other words, the trainer doesn't get to see the dog until the damage has been done.

The best approach the trainer can take is to avoid the fight or rather put it off until he has some way of handling the animal. It is best if the owners can take the dog from their car and put him on a stall chain, leaving the lead attached to the dog's collar. If the owner is afraid to handle the dog, and I have seen this, then you must do as follows. You and your assistant must each lasso the dog so that when he turns to bite you, your assistant will pull him toward himself. You will do the same when the dog goes for your assistant. It is best to attach him to a stall chain. The dog is now confused. He has been handled by total strangers whom he could not back off. Also, now he is alone in a strange environment,

This sequence shows the proper way to hold a dog off if it should turn
to bite the handler during protection work and, otherwise. Regardless
of the dog's twisting and turning, it is unable to bite the handler.

These photos of Mrs. Burke handling a dog offering aggression clearly illustrate some things that should never be done. For example, the left hand should always be held taut, stiff-armed so as to prevent the dog from biting the handler if he should turn in his fury. As can be clearly seen, Ann doesn't have the dog under control and is not prepared to prevent an accident.

away from his pack members; for the first time in his life, no one is afraid of him. You must know that generally a fight between you and this dog is inevitable.

When you teach him obedience, he will probably refuse submission and will challenge. However, you are to ignore his challenges until the right moment. Your first job is to be able to handle him. This will be accomplished in no longer than a few days. You must walk by him and out of his reach, completely ignoring him. This will confuse him. His aggressive attitude toward you will lessen in its intensity, because he is getting used to seeing you and will feel more secure, for he remains unchallenged and remains unafraid. Eventually you will be able to walk by him and receive just a stare. After a short while longer, you will be able to take his lead and walk him, but don't do this unless you are *certain* he will not challenge you. Remember, the fight must be avoided temporarily. Therefore, have your assistant join you in the double lasso (use a rope) and move him in this manner. After handling him a few times, your assistant will no longer be necessary. However, you must see for yourself when the time has come for this step. Don't rush things. Don't feed him that day. Give him only water. Probably he wouldn't eat anyway. The following day, after an 18-hour period has elapsed, the dog will be more ready to tolerate a new pack leader. After walking him, feed him. Then take him for another walk.

It is a good idea to start training this dog by teaching those commands requiring the least compulsion, such as heel and sit. After each successful lesson, you are slowly impressing upon him your ability to lead and to control. His attitude will reflect this. Be certain to always be ready for his challenge from the very start. You are making a com-

The physical capacities of the trainer, coupled with considerations of the size and weight of the dog being trained, play a part in determining training techniques. A challenge rendered by this beautiful harlequin Great Dane, for example, would be a serious challenge indeed! Photo by Louise Van der Meid.

plete attempt to avoid the fight; however, if it should come about, you must be prepared to win at any cost.

The method you employ if and when the fight arises is to hold the dog off and away from you with the lead. You may hang him, swing him about and strike the dowel against the side of his face, but you *must* win the fight when it comes. If you don't think you can win, you must avoid it. Remember, this is a dog who totally believes in his own powers. Chances are that someone is beating him for the first time in his life. However, I have never seen a dog that a man—the *right* man—couldn't handle. The dog must come to respect you completely if he is ever to respect his owners in the future. If you can't impress him with your pack leadership, his life has no future. Therefore, I repeat, do whatever you must, but make him submit.

This photo clearly illustrates what to do if a bad dog should approach or attack you: FREEZE! Don't move at all; it is a very rare dog that will continue to attack an immobile person. This is the best position to adopt by people—including children—who are afraid of dogs.

In my many years of working with many dogs of various breeds, only very few did I consider to be in the category of the above-described dog. My findings were that in almost all cases the fight could be avoided if the dog were handled properly. The few who did challenge submitted in less than one minute and I never had to hang any dog or swing him about. When one did offer a challenge that I finally accepted, I had him at a point of some control. I had already established in his mind that I could handle him, make him sit or heel somewhat—but more important, I had established that I wasn't really a bad guy. Therefore, by holding him off with the lead, a few swats with the switch across the side of the face and nose was all that was necessary. Remember, the longer the fight can be prevented, the better off everyone is.

THE MAD BITER

The most relentless, the most determined biter I have ever worked with was a Lhasa Apso male who was three years old. The man of the house was a traveling salesman, and there were no children in the family. From the time the dog was a little puppy, he would lie in bed next to his mistress whenever the husband was gone on a trip. When the man returned, the dog was forced to sleep at the bottom of the bed or on the floor. The woman had adopted the dog as the child she didn't have. The man played the father role for whatever reason he might have had.

When the dog reached two years old he would without warning and for no reason known to the couple growl at either of them. They didn't understand, but they felt personally guilty. They rationalized that their child had a mind of his own. He continued this pattern for a few months after which time, while the wife was kissing the dog's mouth, the animal bit and ripped open her lower lip, making it necessary for her to receive twelve stitches. Another time, while the man was watching television with his wife seated next to him and the dog in his lap, he proceeded to pat the dog's head. As he did so, without warning the dog bit and ripped open the hand, necessitating eight stitches.

After these occurrences, the problem intensified. The dog would be friendly toward all, strangers as well, but suddenly, without apparent provocation, he would bite and rip.

One time, while the woman was changing clothes, the dog stood at the door and growled at her. When she tried to walk out of the bedroom, he stood fast and growled harder, showing his teeth. She yelled for help and when the husband, who was in the other room, came in the dog walked away and lay down on the floor next to the bed.

When left alone in the house, the dog on occasion would urinate on the side of the mattress where the woman slept. He also would urinate on the man's side. When the couple would have sexual relations, the dog would remain under the bed. The moment the man reached climax, the dog would instantly jump onto the end of the bed.

The foregoing were the facts I managed to learn during my questioning of the couple. The following was my logic and method of training. The first step is to try to understand the dog's actions by going back to the animal within his pack living in the wild. When in this natural environment, dogs urinate as a means of communicating to other animals. Urination as well as defecation are means of marking off territory. They are telling other animals to keep away from their turf. Also, through urination, the males leave their sexual calling cards, so to speak. When we bring the dog into our civilization and domesticate him, his natural means of communication remain the same. He may urinate on every tree or fire hydrant. Even if he has just relieved himself completely, he will still manage to spurt out a few drops. What he is doing is leaving his calling card for bitches in the area. Also, he is claiming territorial rights. After defecation, he will very often use his back feet to dig into the ground beneath him. Again, he is claiming his territorial rights.

The subject dog had urinated on both sides of the mattress, so we could assume that he was claiming both man and woman. The problem had been created by both partners. The woman had no children. She had treated the dog as her child as far as she was concerned, and as far as the dog was concerned the woman had become sexually desirable, especially so after he became aware of the fact that she menstruated. Male dogs can mate only while the bitch is in season. Therefore, this condition is most exciting and stimulating to the male. The fact that he had been made aware of the physiology of the woman, her bleeding, was the original impetus. The dog felt the physical warmth of the woman's body while the man was gone. Upon the man's return, the dog was overpowered by a higher pack member and therefore was forced to assume his subordinate role. The dog had no real pack leader. If he did, the problem would have been nipped at its origin.

As the dog matured, his sexual drive continued to be motivated. Finally, he made his first stand. He growled—and he got away with this overt behavior. He *should* have been corrected instantly. After many such displays of growling, he finally bit the woman's lips. Both this biting and the biting of the man's hand were displays of his sexual frustrations. In reality, he wanted to have sex with both pack members. When dogs copulate, they will rough-house and bite each other during the pre-play or chase.

The biting of the man and woman as well as strangers got worse. With each successful bite, the dog found sexual pleasure. Also, as far as he was concerned, he had succeeded in asserting himself and of moving toward his goal of achieving higher position within the pack. If he could manage to take over as the highest member within the pack, he could satisfy his sexual needs whenever desired.

On the occasion when the dog prevented the woman from leaving her bedroom, he was making a very definite stand. However, he didn't believe that he could overpower the man, who was still above him within the pack, so he took his position at the foot of the bed. He started to bite strangers, thus displaying his aggression. Besides, biting was sexually pleasurable to him; he was asserting himself in the desire to obtain sexual gratification from outside his pack.

Upon the man's reaching sexual climax, the dog knew that he could rejoin his pack in closer physical proximity. Therefore, he jumped back onto the bed. If he had thought he could overpower his other pack members, he would have claimed either member he desired at that moment and not have assumed the position beneath the bed.

My method of training this dog was as follows: The novice might suggest allowing the dog to be mated with another dog. This would not work at all. The dog's imagination had been awakened. He wanted people. After all, it was people who had created his urge, not dogs. He would take a dog, but his desire was for people.

I believe that all dogs are bisexual by nature. In this particular case, the bisexuality had been made to exist for people. The dog wanted to have sex with both the man and the woman. If the problem had gone uncorrected, eventually the dog would have made a much stronger move. He would have tried to mount either the woman or the man—regardless of the size differential involved. When pushed off and away, he would have severely attacked and hurt the person of his affections.

I recall a similar case in which a male German Shepherd came to me to be taught obedience. The dog had displayed no overtly sexual acts to the family as far as they were aware. Their only problem was lack of control. After working with the animal several days, I became aware of his problem, one which luckily was in its early stages: this dog was homosexually attracted to men. He wanted no part of a woman. This was not apparent to most people, because he was very friendly toward women and had displayed aggression on rare occasions only toward men. He was about a year old. After I had explained to the woman that at some unpredictable future moment the dog would mount her husband or her son and that after being pushed away he would attack viciously, the woman called me a screwball and refused to allow me to continue with training her dog. She took him home and employed some other trainer who agreed with the woman, and the dog was taught obedience. Approximately seven months later the woman phoned me and told me of a tragedy: the dog had done just as I had predicted. He mounted the husband and, after being pushed away, he attacked him viciously, giving him wounds that required 120 stitches.

With the Lhasa Apso, the same could have happened to either man or woman. The first step was to castrate the animal. Castration alone, however, is far from sufficient in curing such cases. Castration will generally require three to six months before noticeable psychological change occurs in the animal. It takes that long for the blood chemistry and bodily functions to coordinate and to compensate. During that period the dog would still recall his past desires and would bite. Therefore, he had to be reconditioned. Biting must become a displeasurable memory for him.

With this particular animal, the slingshot and switch was ineffective. If provoked, the dog would bite with rage and completely disregard the marbles hitting his body. Therefore it was necessary to provide the assistant with a circular buffer which he could hold easily between his thumb and index finger. The buffer was small enough to be hidden by the man's hand until the dog started biting. Once biting started, the assistant would allow the dog to bite onto the protruding steel nobs. The dog was so intense in his fury he could continue to bite as he bled. It required three weeks of this type of conditioning, coordinated with use of the slingshot, and obedience work for the dog to become convinced that biting was no longer pleasurable. I advised the people to bring the dog back for further conditioning if the dog should demonstrate even the slightest signs of aggressive behavior. Three days after he returned home, his growling started once again. I told the people to return with their dog. After I had several assistants tease the dog, I quickly determined that reconditioning was not necessary. The dog only growled, but he refused to bite. The people required further schooling in obedience handling so that the owners could assert themselves more completely and thus raise their pack position to that of pack leader. The dog had to be a dog pack member, not a human pack member. This type of relationship had to continue to exist if the dog were to take his proper pack position. If not, regression might have taken place, requiring further reconditioning. It's been several years now and it seems that the pack is doing well.

COMMON PROBLEMS

So many people ask, "What should I do if while walking down the street a dog or a pack of dogs attacks me?" The answer is: freeze. If you don't move, you will not get bitten. By backing away, you induce the dog to vent its hunting instinct and so to chase and to seize its prey with his mouth; 99% of the time, no dog will bite a non-moving person. If he does bite, he won't sink in his teeth as long as the person remains still.

Car Sickness: Car or motion sickness often is caused by psychological reasons in many dogs. These animals generally have come to associate the car with unpleasant endings such as a visit to the veterinarian. Psychological upset is the only one of many possible causes. Others might be the physical feel of the car itself, the smell of the fumes or possibly the awareness of the potential danger of this great machine which the pack leader communicates to the dog through body odors.

This problem can generally be resolved through positive experiences. For example, you can sit with the dog in the parked car and feed him by hand. This should be attempted and continued until the dog accepts the food readily and no longer drools. When excessive salivation—which almost always precedes car sickness—stops and the dog accepts food, you will notice a marked difference in the attitude of the animal in regard to entering the car. After this has been accomplished, short rides ending in happy experiences should be repeated daily. The rides should increase in time very gradually, and always the master should attempt to end each trip before the animal vomits. The first several trips might last only one minute. At the end of each ride, dog and master should enter into dog pack play, accompanied by the offering of favorite treats.

The time necessary to overcome car sickness varies with the individual animal. Some dogs will come to enjoy the car in several days, and others will require months of positive conditioning.

In some cases, the motion sickness is caused by continuous stimulation of the receptors in the labyrinth of the dog's inner ear as a result of stopping, starting and turning. Very often veterinarians will prescribe drug therapy to prevent the condition.

Dog Care

One big job of any dog owner is to clean, clean and do more cleaning. Our aim must be to prevent disease and sickness. Cleanliness is the best method. Soap, hot water, a good brush, a strong back and strong knees are prerequisites for any kennel man. The person owning one or two dogs of course has less cleaning to do.

If prevention isn't successful, you have to be able to recognize symptoms of illness at their very start so that veterinary supervision can begin as quickly as possible.

Every dog owner should be aware that dogs are much like people in giving evidence of their sicknesses. In most cases illnesses show themselves by causing in the affected dog visible signs of the results of the physical changes being worked in the animal. Sick dogs usually look sick; you have to learn what to look for and to recognize which ailments are related to specific symptoms. Different parts of the dog's body present different evidences of the results of disease, so I'll cover them separately.

COAT

The dog's coat should have luster and a healthy, clean sheen. Visible conditions suggesting problems are: 1) Dry coat; 2) Dandruff; 3) Excessive scratching; 4) Missing hairs; 5) Lesions; 6) Crusted

All types of anti-parasite products and preparations are available at pet shops to keep dogs safe from the parasites like fleas and ticks and lice that commonly attack them. Remember that keeping your dog free of parasites is not done merely to relieve him of annoyance; in many cases parasite infestation can be severe enough to completely debilitate the dog and make him susceptible to other parasites and diseases.

areas; 7) Scaling; 8) Red or irritated patches or sores; 9) Growths or lumps.

The coat should be inspected regularly in search of external parasites such as ticks and fleas. These parasites most generally harbor themselves behind and inside the ears, under the neck, in the anal area and where the legs join the body. However, they can be found on any part of the dog's body.

When any mentioned irregularity is observed, the dog should be taken to a veterinarian immediately. The DVM should do a skin scraping and examine it closely under the microscope in order to correctly diagnose the problem. Only then can proper treatment be given.

EYE DISORDERS

The dog's eyes should be clear and full of life. Any irregularity should be checked instantly. Symptoms of eye disorders are: 1) Inflammation of the conjunctiva, or eyelids; 2) Running eyes; 3) Pus in the eyes; 4) Crustiness on lids; 5) Abnormal thickness of lids; 6) Swelling of the eyelids; 7) Inversion of the lids; 8) Irritation of the cornea; 9) Prolapse of the third eyelid; 10) Enlargement of the tissue at the corner of the eye. This is common in young dogs; 11) Abnormal coloring or lines or spots in the cornea.

EAR DISORDERS

Symptoms of ear disorders are: 1) Scratching and self-mutilation; 2) Sores and scratches; 3) Redness, irritation; 4) Growths.

Dogs with flapping ears, such as many of the hound breeds, are more prone to ear infections. The ears of every dog should be checked and cleaned regularly.

INFECTIOUS DISEASES

Dogs are susceptible to at least 100 types of virus infection. The best means of prevention known presently is vaccination. All puppies at eight and ten weeks of age should receive temporary DHL inoculations. At 12 weeks of age, their bodies are ready to accept permanent immunity and so should receive permanent inoculation. At six months of age, the puppy should receive rabies inoculation. Thereafter, the dog should be re-inoculated at least once a year. If your dog has other duties besides being a house pet, that is, if he often comes into contact with strange dogs, he should receive booster shots every six months in my opinion.

The symptoms of viral infections should be treated immediately in the hope of preventing secondary infection. Common symptoms of viral infections are: 1) Running eyes; 2) Running nose—white discharge; 3) Coughing; 4) Red throat; 5) Fever; 6) Loss of appetite; 7) Listlessness; 8) Enlarged tonsils; 9) Intense thirst; 10) Diarrhea; 11) Blood in the excrement; 12) Muscle stiffness; 13) Rigidity of the tail; 14) Stiffness in gaiting; 15) Vomiting.

The moment any of these symptoms appears, you are to consult a veterinarian immediately. Time is of the essence.

I have found that a close watch of the dog's stool generally provides a good indication as to the animal's general condition. A loose or poorly shaped stool, if it persists, should be checked out. Internal parasites, change of diet, nervousness, excessive water intake or a variety of other causes can be responsible. It is an excellent idea and preventive measure to have your veterinarian examine your dog's stool every few months. Regardless, at the onset of any of these symptoms or warning signals, you should immediately consult a veterinarian.

DISORDERS OF THE DIGESTIVE SYSTEM

Symptoms of disorders in the digestive system are: 1) Growths in the lips; 2) Excessive salivation for the individual animal; 3) Reluctance to eat or drink; 4) Pain when moving the jaw, lips or tongue; 5) Malodorous breath; 6) Inflamed tissue about the teeth; 7) Swollen and/or painful tongue; 8) Inflamed, tender gums; 9) Bleeding gums; 10) Loose teeth; 11) Expulsion of white, frothy mucoid material or mucus from the throat; 12) Pain when swallowing; 13) Coughing; 14) Fever; 15) Vomiting; 16) Re-swallowing; 17) Tiredness or listlessness; 18) Constipation; 19) Emaciation; 20) Dehydration; 21) Blood in vomit or stool or urine; 22) Worms or their eggs appearing in the stool. A preventive of internal parasites in the kennel is use of sodium borate at the rate of 10 1/100 sq. ft. or saturated aqueous solutions of sodium chloride at the rate of 1 gal/ 10 sq. ft. applied to the runs. Fecal examination should be done regularly to discover parasites at an early stage; 23) Watery or soft bowel movements of increased frequency; 24) Straining when defecating; 25) Perforated, web-like appearance on the skin around the anus; 26) Frequent biting at the anal region; 27) Indigestion; 28) Pain in the animal when it is picked up; 29) Undigested fats in the stool; 30) Loss of weight; 31) Weakness, disorientation or confusion and panting. Trembling. Spasmodic twitching of the muscles. Convulsions. This is generally an indication of pancreatic trouble.

The digestive system consists of lips, mouth, teeth, pharynx, esophagus, stomach, small and large intestine, pancreas, liver, anus and rectum. All of these places can provide symptoms of disorder. Any of the described symptoms are indicative of any one of a number of possible disorders and should be checked out medically.

HEART DISEASE

The best preventive approach is regular visits to your veterinarian, who will examine the dog's cardiovascular system.

DIABETES

Urine analysis should be done by your veterinarian regularly. This will indicate the blood sugar level and proper care if necessary may be started.

Symptoms of diabetes are: 1) Emaciation although food consumption frequently is increased; 2) Bilateral cataracts; 3) Nocturia; 4) Weakness; 5) Acidosis; 6) Depression; 7) Dehydration; 8) Extreme thirst; 9) Anxiety—nervousness; 10) Passing out.

GENERAL NUTRITION

I specified in the chapter dealing with housebreaking what I consider to be a good diet. However, each animal is an individual, and the causes of malnutrition are therefore many—different dogs will be malnourished for different reasons.

Every system in an animal must receive a required nutrient to the point of ultimate use. These nutrients must be available in proper amount and in proper sequence to adequately support the essential metabolic processes of the dog. If not, malnutrition will exist.

The major symptoms of malnutrition are obesity, tiredness, poor coat, general run down condition and emaciation. Malnutrition in dogs can be caused by physiological problems peculiar to the individual dog, pathological conditions and the owner's ignorance about what and when to feed.

If your dog shows any symptom or doesn't seem to do well on the commercially prepared diet you feed or after using the diet I have outlined in the housebreaking chapter, consult your veterinarian.

RESPIRATORY TRACT OBSTRUCTION

Symptoms of obstruction of the respiratory tract are: 1) Mouth breathing; 2) Persistent sneezing accompanied by nasal discharge from one side of the nose; 3) Gagging; 4) Expectoration of phlegm; 5) Snoring; 6) Hacking cough; 7) Nasal discharge with or without blood; 8) Retching; 9) Vomiting; 10) Rapid and shallow respirations. If any of these symptoms is present, consult your veterinarian.

DISEASES OF THE UROGENITAL SYSTEM

Symptoms of disease in the urogenital system are: 1) Depression; 2) Vomiting; 3) Diarrhea; 4) Rise in temperature sometimes—only in cases of bacterial or viral infections. However, the body temperature is usually normal or subnormal; 5) Pain in the kidney region; 6) Scanty urine flow at times; 7) Foul breath; 8) Weight loss; 9) Digestive upsets; 10) Listlessness; 11) Weakness; 12) Nervousness; 13) Increased thirst; 14) Abdominal enlargement; 15) Lumbar pain; 16) Straining to urinate; 17) Frequent urination becoming uncontrollable; 18) Blood in the urine; 19) Walking in a crouched position.

VAGINITUS AND VULVITIS

Symptoms of vaginitus and vulvitis are: 1) Licking of the part; 2) Straining; 3) Vaginal discharge; 4) Odor.

PSEUDOPREGNANCY (FALSE PREGNANCY)

False pregnancy usually occurs from five to ten weeks after the bitch's receptive phase during heat. The symptoms are: 1) Enlarged and engorged mammary glands with lactation; 2) Slight abdominal distension; 3) Swelling and relaxation of the vulva, and relaxation of the pelvic ligaments; 4) "nest-making or making of beds," which often includes hiding in closets or under furniture, tearing up clothing or papers; 5) "Nursing" toys, bones, slippers or other inanimate objects and displaying aggressive protective behavior if the owner attempts to remove them; 6) Vomiting or diarrhea; 7) Self-nursing; 8) Subnormal body temperature. Consult your veterinarian for treatment.

In regard to the last statement about consulting your veterinarian for treatment, the rule of course is a good one to follow in **any** case in which you suspect that abnormal behavior on the dog's part has been caused by an injury or illness. When abnormal behavior persists, your veterinarian is your first line of defense in protecting your dog. Some dog owners erroneously insist on trying to doctor their dogs, and both the dogs and they eventually pay the price for their shortsightedness.

INJURIES TO THE NERVOUS SYSTEM

The spinal cord of the dog is easily injured. Treatment should take place immediately after the accident in order to obtain best results.

Symptoms of disorder in the nervous system are: 1) Pain; 2) Rigidity or spastic paralysis; 3) Arched back; 4) Crying or whining; 5) Resistance to handling; 6) Muscular spasms; 7) Reluctance to move; 8) Weakness.

ARTHRITIS (THE INFLAMMATION OF A JOINT)

Generally, strains and sprains are the most common causes of acute traumatic arthritis. If the condition is not corrected from the start, permanent damage may result.

HIP DYSPLASIA

Hip dysplasia is a genetic condition characterized by faulty development of the hip joint. Symptoms are: 1) Hip dysplasia may be present without overt signs. Therefore, when suspected, x-rays should be taken; 2) Hip lameness before or after exercise; 3) Reluctance to rise from a resting position; 4) Evidence of pain and stiffness when first beginning to move after rest; 5) A foreleg lameness may result from abnormal weight distribution in an attempt to relieve hip stress; 6) The hindquarters may appear "boxy."

Modern medicine has advanced to such a degree that this condition very often can be corrected through surgery.

SPRAINS

A sprain is a temporary displacement of two opposing joint surfaces and is associated with partial or complete tearing of some of the supporting ligaments of the joint involved. There is a brief sharp pain at the moment of injury, followed by a consistent aching pain that might persist for many days. The dog will generally hold up his leg, the most usual area of sprain. The involved part is extremely tender and swells rapidly. There is increased heat in the area.

Treatment—immediately apply cold ice packs and consult your veterinarian.

THE COUGH

Coughing is not a disease but merely a sign of a disease; it may be mild yet it may be serious enough to cause death.

Diseases in which cough is a prominent sign usually fall into one of four general categories.

1) Diseases involving multiple systems, such as distemper; 2) Diseases of the respiratory system, such as bronchitis and bronchietosis; 3) Diseases of the cardiovascular system, such as heartworm; 4) Diseases of the upper digestive system, such as the occasional foreign body. The cough should be checked out instantly with your veterinarian.

FLATULENCE

Flatulence is the expulsion by belching or passing through the rectum of an excessive accumulation of gas in the stomach or intestines. A bland diet might serve to rectify the problem; if this condition persists, however, a veterinarian should be consulted to prevent acute gastric flatulence.

The Concept of Trick Work

The variance in capacity to perform a given trick arises partly from the temperament of the dog concerned—not all dogs of a given size can perform the same tricks—and partly from the strictly physical considerations involved. The breeds vary in physical makeup; they have different sizes and weights, different angulation of the legs, different facial and dental configurations. German Shepherds, St. Bernards and Dachshunds, for example, are not physically equipped to walk or to dance on their hind legs. Consequently, it would be foolish to attempt to teach them to do so, for it would only serve to agonize the animal. And of course you wouldn't expect an English Bulldog to jump five feet vertically into the air in order to take a telephone receiver into his mouth, remove it from its cradle and then to return to his master with the receiver in his mouth.

Consequently, before attempting any trick, you must evaluate the physical capabilities of the individual dog. Also, you must quickly evaluate the dog's psychological aptitude for each trick by the attitude he displays after he understands what is expected from him. Unlike obedience work, which every normal dog can be taught, trick work requires that the dog have a special talent for the particular trick.

Trick work also requires inducements far more compelling in nature then all other types of training.

Consequently, the dog becomes more submissive to you, his pack leader, thus making him a more dependent animal with a tighter bond to you. The fun the two of you will share will only serve to enrich your relationship, he as pack member and you as pack leader possessing despotic power.

DOING THE ZIG-ZAG

For this trick, you need a dog physically capable of walking in and out between your legs. His height must not exceed the bottom of your groin.

To start, the dog should be at your left side in the automatic sit position. A handle or rope should be attached to the loop of his prong collar. Hold onto the handle and take one step forward with your right foot. As you do so, say "**Zig-zag**" and simultaneously gently pull or push him through your legs. After his entire body has passed between your legs, praise and give food.

Now hold the handle in your left hand and step forward with your left foot. At that moment say "**Zig-zag**" and simultaneously snap the collar gently so that the dog walks through your legs again. If he rebels against the gentle snap, pull or push him through and then praise and feed. Continue with this procedure for one more right and left step.

Allow the dog to rest for a few minutes, and then repeat the exercise, stopping after 5 to 10 minutes. End the session by putting your dog through the obedience paces. He should know them well enough for you to be able to end the session with the dog's having been successful at working with the pack leader. . . a good confidence-builder.

The following day, repeat the zig-zag procedure. After a while the dog will come to understand that each time your right foot moves forward, he is compelled to pass through your legs. Then your left

Attaching the short loop handle prior to teaching the Zig-zag trick.

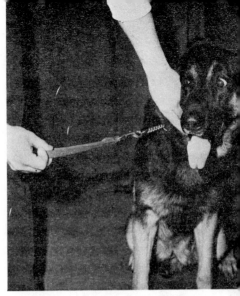

Below: the dog passes through the legs when the right leg is extended and then passes through them again when the left leg is extended. The loop handle is always held in the hand corresponding to the extended leg.

After completion of Zig-zag training, the dog readily performs the trick without any attachment to his collar and without the need for any pushing or pulling to get him through your legs. The Zig-zag trick may not be very exciting to watch, but it's easy for the dog to learn and the owner to teach and therefore serves as a good basis for teaching other tricks.

foot moves forward, and again he passes through. Once he seems to get the gist of it, as evidenced by his moving slowly through your legs without too much inducement, it is time to offer stronger compulsion. With each step, snap the handle. Don't do any more pulling or pushing of the dog through your legs. A few sharp snaps will increase his velocity. Take four successive steps; with the right step forward, use your right hand to snap the handle—with the left step, use your left hand to snap the handle. Upon completion of four steps, praise the dog lavishly and offer a food reward. Practice for five to ten minutes. Again, end each session with fun such as dog pack play.

After several days of this conditioning, let go of the handle. Simply step forward and say "**Zig-zag**." Take a left step forward and repeat "**Zig-zag**." Take another right and left step in the same manner. Each time the dog hesitates, reach down and snap the handle, thus compelling him to go through. He will soon be conditioned to know that each time you step forward and say "**Zig-zag**" he is to pass through.

This is a relatively simple trick that most dogs can master. Once they understand it, they will love doing it.

JUMPING OVER THE STICK

Any dog can be taught to jump. Some dogs of course have more physical ability to jump than others, so the heights attained will vary with the talent and size of the individual animal.

No dog should be taught to jump until he is at least eight months old. The front shoulders should be fairly well developed so as to be strong enough to support the dog's body weight when he lands on his front paws.

Place a broomstick about three feet long on the floor and induce the dog to walk over it by gently snapping the lead and you walk over with him. Each time you and the dog step over, say "**Hup**" and gently snap the lead to provide inducement.

After each completion, praise lavishly and offer food. After several repetitions the dog will enjoy walking over the stick and no inducement other than the word "Hup" will be necessary.

At this point, hold the stick about an inch off the ground in your right hand. Hold the lead in your left hand, say "**Hup**" and simultaneously snap the lead,

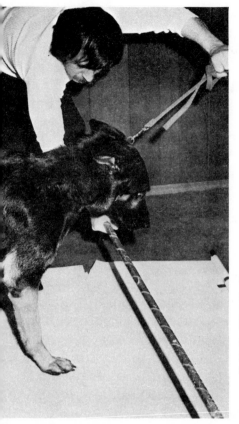

With the lead held in his left hand and the stick in his right, just a short distance above the floor, the trainer encourages the dog to jump by saying "Hup" and snapping the lead in the direction of the jump.

compelling the dog to jump over. If he refuses, force him to go over by pulling him with the lead. As his feet hit the floor, immediately turn him about by using the lead and repeat "**Hup**," simultaneously snapping the lead toward you, thus compelling his return jump. When he has completed the jump, praise him lavishly and give food reward. Repeat this several times until the dog goes over two or three times on his own without your having to snap the lead. At this point, become a pack member and dog play with him.

If you ever decide to teach your dog utility degree obedience work, part of the requirement will be to jump the hurdle, retrieve the dumb-bell and return over the hurdle. We are conditioning him for the return jump with this exercise.

The following day, repeat the exercise with the stick held one inch off the ground. After two or three successful jumps, raise the height of the stick by an inch. Repeat the same procedure of compulsion and reward. After two or three more successful jumps, engage once again in dog play. Then review something he already knows, and stop the lesson. You as the trainer should try to make all this a game by giving the command "**Hup**" in a high, happy voice; follow each successful jump with a lot of play.

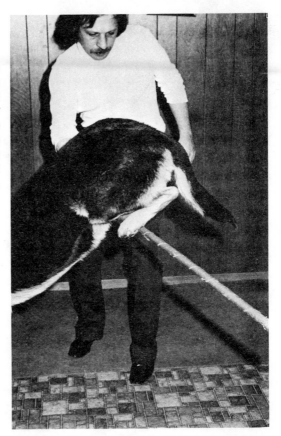

Training progresses slowly, with the stick being raised in height above the floor gradually. Here the dog is making the return jump without any handle attached to his collar.

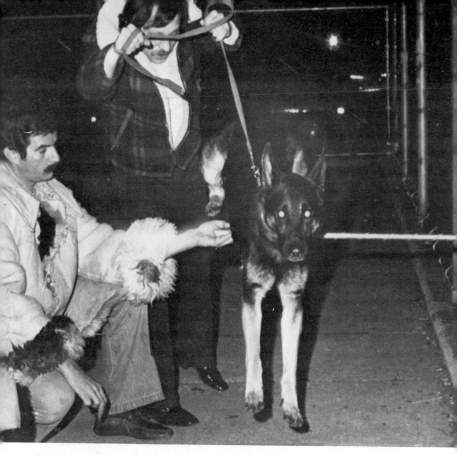

Employing an assistant and a chain link fence to encourage the dog to jump greater heights than he can jump indoors without a running start.

The following day, review the one-inch and the two-inch jump two or three times each. Then raise the height of the stick to three inches and repeat the same procedure. Never continue to work the dog on any trick after he has succeeded two or three times. Therefore, each lesson should not exceed 15 minutes in duration.

Continue to raise the height of the stick gradually. You will eventually reach a height that the dog can't seem to clear regardless of the inducement. At this point, lower the height so that the dog ends the lesson successfully.

Some dogs, after gaining an understanding of what is expected by the inducement word "hup," have a tendency to drop their hindquarters as they jump over the stick. To rectify the problem, lightly tap the stick into the hocks of the lagging hind legs as he jumps. This will induce him to raise his hind legs when jumping.

When the dog reaches a height that he just can't seem to clear, employ an assistant. Have the helper place the end of a broomstick four to five feet long into a chain link fence so that one end of the stick is supported by the fencing and the other end by the helper. First have the dog jump a low height while you induce him with the lead. After a few repetitions, the dog will jump over the stick and back without your having to snap the lead. Now raise the stick to a height you feel he can jump if induced.

From the automatic sit position, with the stick about four or five feet away, start to run toward the stick with the dog at your side. As the dog approaches the stick, say "**Hup**" and employ the lead to induce the animal to jump over and back. If he clears it, try a higher jump. When you reach a height that seems too much for the dog, stop. Go back to a successful jump and end the lesson. Remember. . . end each session with dog pack play and food and fun.

JUMPING THE HURDLE

The height that seemed to stifle the animal with the stick can be cleared with the hurdle.

Starting with a low height, employing the same procedure as with the stick as regards inducement and reinforcements, have the dog jump. After several days, he will be jumping the hurdle to and fro. Now, raise the height to the desired goal. Stand at the opposite side of the hurdle, lead in hand and facing the dog, who is sitting. Say "**Hup**" and simultaneously snap the lead to you. If the dog falters, pull him over so that he is successful. When he reaches you, praise him and offer food. Leave him in the sit-stay position and return to the other side of the hurdle. Again repeat the procedure. When he eventually clears the hurdle, make him jump over and return without using the lead. Make certain to end each lesson with the dog's successfully jumping the hurdle regardless of the height. He must be the winner.

Don't push the dog beyond his capabilities. As time passes, if he is exercised at jumping every day, his muscular development will increase and so will the heights he is able to achieve.

JUMPING THROUGH THE HOOP

Any normal dog can jump through a hoop; only the height of the hoop he can jump through depends upon his individual talent.

To start, hold the lead in your right hand. The dog is either in a sit-stay or standing position. Hold the hoop (a bicycle tire makes a good hoop) in your left hand, facing the dog. One part of the hoop should rest on the floor. The lead is extended through the hoop. Say "**Hup**" and gently snap the lead, inducing the dog to walk through. After several repetitions, he will no longer fear this strange hoop and will walk through without hesitation. After each passing through the hoop, praise and offer food reward.

The next day, repeat the same procedure. After he walks through the hoop two or three times, raise it one inch off the ground. From a sit-stay position, say "**Hup**" and simultaneously snap the lead, inducing the dog to jump through. After he lands,

With the hoop resting on the floor and the lead extended through it, the lead is snapped toward the trainer, inducing the dog to pass through. After a few repetitions of this procedure, the dog learns that the hoop—which is at first a fairly sinister-looking object to him—holds no fears for him.

praise him and immediately snap him back through the hoop. Offer food. Do this until he responds simply to the word inducement "hup." After two or three successful jumps, end the lesson as previously described.

Continue with this procedure each day until the dog jumps a desired height and does so without your having to snap the lead. Now take off the lead. If the dog is not successful, return to using the lead until he reaches a point of conditioning and confidence that enables him to achieve success with no lead. He must perform merely upon hearing the word "hup" and seeing the hoop.

Some dogs will have a tendency to drop their back legs when going through the hoop. If this occurs, merely rotate the bottom of the hoop so that it contacts the dog's hocks as he jumps through. He will quickly learn to keep his back legs up.

JUMPING THROUGH THE ARMS

The same procedure as with the hoop is employed.

The dog is in a sit-stay position. Have an assistant hold the lead so that it passes through your arms, which you hold open in the form of a ring. The

Teaching the dog to jump through your arms is a logical progression from teaching him to jump through the hoop. With the dog in a sit-stay position and an assistant holding the lead so that it extends from the dog through your arms, keep your back towards the dog but crane your neck so that you're facing him.

As the dog jumps through your arms, you turn your face in the direction he's going so that there is no chance for a collision. Here Buddy, an accomplished performer, jumps on command and without any lead attached to his collar.

assistant is facing the dog. You are standing between the dog and the assistant. Your back is to the dog but your head is turned so that you are facing the dog and peering at him through your open arms.

Hold your open arms at a height that you are sure the dog can jump. Say "**Hup**" and simultaneously have the assistant snap the lead toward himself, forcing the dog to go through your arms. The first several attempts will be the hardest, for the dog is fearful of physically coming into this type of bodily contact with his pack leader. However, the assistant must physically snap and pull the dog through. As the dog approaches your open arms, turn your head forward. If you don't, his face will collide with yours. Immediately after the dog passes through your arms, you are to praise him lavishly. After several successful moves through your arms, the dog will cease to be fearful and will jump through with the slightest inducement from the lead.

The following day, repeat the procedure. After a short while, the dog will jump through without being snapped. At this point, take off the lead. In a high excited voice say "**Good puppy.**" Place the dog in a sit-stay position and excitedly say "**Hup.**" The dog will jump through your arms. Try to help him as he attempts it. Afterward, needless to say, praise and offer food. After two or three successful jumps, stop the lesson.

Repeat this two or three times every day. Also repeat hoop-, stick- and hurdle-jumping two or three times each day. It will become a great game to the dog. He will enjoy it and will steadily improve. But remember that you yourself must inspire the dog through a happy and excited attitude after each successful attempt.

Another method of teaching the dog to jump through your arms after he has learned the hoop jump is to place the dog in a sit-stay position backed up in a corner of the room. He must not be able to back up even one step. Offer your ring-shaped or hoop-shaped arms and move backward toward the dog. As your *open* arms circle his head, say "**Hup**" and continue to back up. The dog has no place to go except through your arms, especially if someone is available to gently snap the lead to compel him to jump.

Regardless of the method that suits you best, always remember to be strong, but also be kind and sensitive to your dog. Don't push him. Make it a game.

RETRIEVING

The dog's natural instinct is to chase animals that run from it, bite them ferociously upon capture and then kill them. A dog will devour his victim if he is hungry, but before doing so he will often drag or carry it to a hiding place. Dogs who have to hunt to survive will drag their prey or some part of it back to their pups.

All dogs pursue their companions, in play, as if they were their prey, and they will do the same with inanimate objects such as a ball or dumb-bell that rolls away. We take advantage of this natural instinct in teaching a dog to retrieve, but we also must call upon his submissive and pack instincts to help. The trainer employs the dog's natural behavior to teach human requirements.

In retrieving, the dog must bring his prey or prey-image (the dumb-bell) or whatever back to the trainer and give it up to him. The dog must do this with objects the smell, taste and weight of which are not necessarily congenial. Therefore, a strict form of compulsion is indispensable if reliable performance is to be obtained. The degree of compulsion of course varies with the individual dog who is being taught to retrieve; sometimes strict compulsion must be applied from the very start. Practiced as a game, however, retrieving is most educational and fun for the novice trainer. Consequently, retrieving in play should always be the method employed by the novice, especially since the object of training can be thereby achieved. If your aim is merely to throw a ball or a wooden object and have the dog chase after it, seize it, return with it and then release it to you, with many dogs the play method will succeed. Unfortunately, the play method doesn't always work.

If your aim is to achieve *real* retrieving, such as selecting the correct answer to a math problem by picking up exactly the correct number (probably the highest degree of training and retrieving), there is no substitute for strict compulsion. When trained under the game method, many dogs will not progress; even if your aim is merely to chase, capture and return, strict compulsion will be the only means to success.

Those who try to teach retrieving as a game must not confront the dog as a pack-leader, but rather as a pack companion of the dog; attempts must be made to stimulate the animal as a playmate, with both man and dog playing with the same prey-image.

The trainer must first decide how to put the dog into the right mood for a game. A dog who is not a pack member or who does not have a strong relationship with the trainer and does not completely trust the trainer can not be put into the proper mood. Also, the dog who has just eaten a big meal or is suffering from thirst, hunger, fatigue or some other disability will be difficult to influence. These internal stimuli are most important.

The game must not take place in an environment where the dog has undergone strict compulsion previously. He will remember those incidents and thus will not take on the proper mood. When selecting the game area, be certain that it is one from which no previous compulsions can be recollected by the animal. An outdoor area can be selected, providing the place chosen is not one that holds distractions which may excite the dog more powerfully than the prey-image. The animal must be prevented from becoming aware of other dogs or cats whether by sight, scent or hearing. We must remember that retrieving entails only the seizure of inanimate prey-images.

One's success when employing this approach will largely depend upon the dog's individual character, past experience and inheritance. Hounds, for example, generally would have more of a natural inclination toward this type of work. When employing strict compulsion, success should be obtained with almost every dog regardless of breed.

AUDITORY SIGNAL—"TAKE IT"

We must first spell out our aim, which is this: from a sitting or standing posture at the left side of the trainer the dog, on recieving an auditory signal, is to run to the object thrown, take or seize it immediately without trying to crush it, and return at a run to the trainer by the shortest route. The dog is then to sit facing the trainer, holding the object in its jaws, until the trainer, by auditory signal, causes it to be given up.

After the dog has learned to take the object upon command and to hold it and not to release it until given auditory signal to do so, upon another command he will be taught to "fetch it" or "find it" and return to the master holding it in his jaws until given an auditory signal to release it.

Our aim is to awaken the instinct of the chase in the dog by movements both of the dumb-bell and of ourselves, thus arousing the desire to seize it. Rapidly moving the dumb-bell to and fro in front of the dog but not close enough for him to snatch it will serve as the primary inducement. The dog is to be

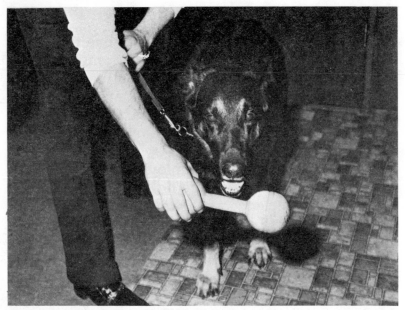

The first step in teaching the retrieve is to arouse the dog's curiosity about the dumb-bell. After the dog has exhibited his curiosity and has made an attempt to get his mouth on it, give it to him, making sure that the insertion of the dumb-bell into the mouth is not painful for the dog.

allowed, not forced, to take it when you see the correct moment has arrived. The trainer must act like a dog who has possession of prey his playmate would like to have.

The dumb-bell is brought from behind the trainer's back, touched against the dog's body and moved about before his eyes. Then it is pulled away and hidden again. You now have the dog's attention. At this point the trainer taps the dumb-bell on the ground a few times, then taps it against the dog's side and quickly withdraws it and runs a few paces away, encouraging the dog to chase by saying "**Good puppy.**" When the dog leaps forward the dumb-bell should be quickly put between his jaws behind his lower canines.

The beginning position for forcing the reluctant dog to open his mouth and accept the dumb-bell. The upper jaw is grasped with the left hand while the fingers exert inward pressure of the mouth's inner tissue against his teeth, thus compelling him to keep his mouth open. The same method is used when forcing a dog to take prescribed medications.

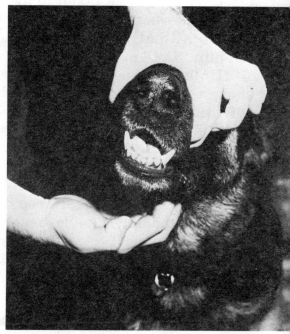

The length of time the dog holds the dumb-bell is increased gradually by holding the bottom jaw closed while keeping your hand in front of his face while you offer verbal encouragement for him to keep the dumb-bell.

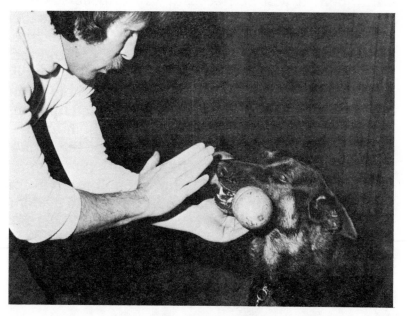

Care should be taken to avoid causing the dog any pain when inserting the dumb-bell into his mouth. At that very moment, caress his head and tell him "**Good puppy**."

If the animal does not open his jaws wide enough, the upper jaw should be gently grasped with the left hand while the thumb, the index finger and the middle fingers of the right hand are discreetly inserted between the jaws with appropriate pressure applied to make the jaws open. As soon as the jaws open, the dumb-bell is to be placed inside the mouth and the fingers removed; the left hand should immediately slide beneath the lower jaw, gently keeping it closed as you praise "good puppy." The dumb-bell should be kept inside the dog's mouth for only a few seconds while a continuous caressing of "good puppy" and head-patting takes place. If the animal tries to open its jaws, allow it to do so. There is no suggestion of compulsion at this point. Repeat this exercise, extending the period of holding the dumb-bell very gradually.

If the dog demonstrates reluctance to taking the dumb-bell, it will be necessary to impose stronger inducement by using your fingers to press harder against his upper lip so that it presses harder against his teeth. He must come to understand that upon hearing the words "**Take it**," it is far more pleasurable to open his mouth and to take hold of the dumb-bell than to feel the pressure exerted upon his upper jaw. The praise and caressing which are immediately given upon his taking hold of the dumb-bell will serve to reinforce this conditioning.

To induce the animal to hold the dumb-bell for longer periods of time (remember, this is to be done very gradually), it is necessary to hold his bottom jaw gently closed with your left hand while placing your right hand in front of his face as you continue

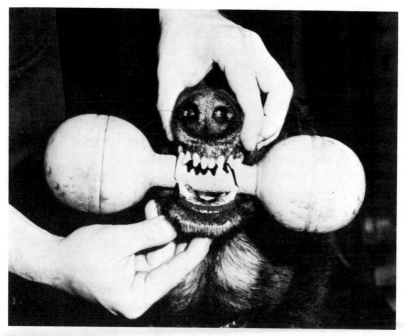

Pressing the dog's lips against his upper teeth (coincidental with giving the "Out" command) while holding your right hand ready to accept the dumb-bell will induce him to release the dumb-bell to you.

to repeat "good puppy." This procedure of course is suggestive of compulsion, which is necessary with certain dogs. Stronger compulsion will be discussed and described later.

OUT —GIVING UP THE DUMB-BELL

Once the dog takes the dumb-bell into his mouth on his own accord, the inducement to cause him to release the dumb-bell upon auditory signal is to begin. As you say "**Out**," gently press the animal's upper lips against his teeth, causing his mouth to open. As he does so, gently take the dumb-bell from his mouth with your right hand and give him praise. Once the dog immediately responds to the word "out," it is important to prevent him from anticipating your command and therefore dropping the article as your right hand moves toward his mouth. To prevent this, frequently move the hand toward his jaws without taking the dumb-bell away. If he drops it, you are to instantly take hold of his upper lips with your left hand and press in as you re-insert the dumb-bell and repeat "Take it." Then give praise and repeat the operation. Eventually the dog will come to concentrate only on the word "out."

TAKING THE DUMB-BELL FROM THE GROUND

Learning to take the dumb-bell from the ground is accomplished gradually. The first step is to accustom the dog to taking the object to the right, left and in front of him as low to the ground as possible. The trainer as previously described is to move the dumb-bell to and fro, inspiring the chase instinct; as he arouses the dog he is to say "Take it," a command which the dog already knows. As the oral signal to seize the dumb-bell is spoken, the trainer is to move the object away from the dog. If the dog reaches down and grasps hold, praise him lavishly. If the dog doesn't respond as desired, apply pressure to the upper lip as previously was described and pull the dog down with the lead as you compel him to take hold.

Once the dog immediately responds and takes hold of the dumb-bell upon "take it," proceed in the following manner.

Allow the dumb-bell to drop from your hand at a moment when it is moving close to the ground and the dog is ready to jump at it. As the dumb-bell rolls along the ground, the trainer says "Take it," uttered in a caressing tone which will further encourage the animal to pick it up. As soon as the dog has the dumb-bell in his jaws a primary inducement for recall is employed. The trainer, who is facing the dog, instantly runs a few paces backwards and calls the dog. If the dog drops the dumb-bell, the trainer is to instantly approach the dog, pick up the dumb-bell and say "Take it" as he applies finger pressure upon the upper lip of the dog. Then praise the dog to offer reassurance and coax him to you by using the proper inducements and continuing to repeat "Take it" as the dog approaches. Upon arrival, remove the dumb-bell by giving the signal "out" and praise.

It must be remembered that not all dogs are natural retrievers. Therefore it will be necessary to offer inducements and compulsions to take the article and to release it at a degree directly proportional to the requirements of the individual animal. The important thing to remember is that upon hearing the words "take it," the dog will respond instantly and reliably only when he realizes that it is more pleasurable to hold the article in his jaws than to feel the inducement to do so. Also, it is far more pleasurable to hold the article until hearing the word "out" than to feel the inducement. How you apply the inducements depends on the needs of the individual animal and the sensitivities of the trainer in regard to application. It is far kinder to offer several sharp effective inducements than very many ineffective ones.

Once you place the dumb-bell on the ground, the dog will either take it upon command or obviously refuse. If he refuses, you may take either of two different approaches. The first is to run to the dumb-bell and kick it so that it starts to roll, thus arousing the dog's chase instinct. As you do so, in a happy and excited voice say "Take it." This method is to continue until the dog takes it without your having to make the article roll. Some dogs, however, will not take it unless they are compelled to do so. For these dogs it is necessary to employ the use of the prong collar. When the dog refuses to take the dumb-bell lying on the ground, as you induce him by saying "**Take it**" you must also compel him to do so by snapping your lead downward so that his mouth moves to the dumb-bell while at the very same instant you apply finger pressure upon his upper lip. When he takes it, praise him accordingly.

Strict compulsion consists of two parts: the first is mechanically bringing the dog's jaws within the snapping range of the desired article, and the second part is causing the jaws to open. This method should be applied as coordinatedly and as simultaneously as possible.

Once the dog has the dumb-bell in his mouth, the trainer is to caress the dog's head with loving

Compelling the dog to pick the dumb-bell up from the floor by applying finger pressure on his upper jaw while his head is forced down.

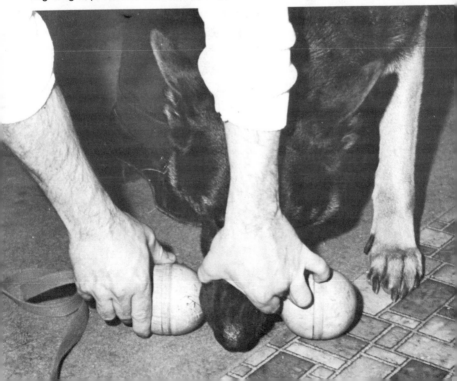

and gentle stroking as he praises "**Good puppy.**" If the dog drops the dumb-bell, instantly the trainer is to snap at the collar, compelling the dog to re-take it. The dog will quickly realize that it is more pleasurable to hold onto the dumb-bell than to drop it.

Once the dog understands, you may proceed by walking with him slowly and cautiously. If he drops the dumb-bell, strict compulsion is to be applied at the moment of dropping, and then a few more steps taken. After two or three successful attempts, stop the lesson. This rule should be applied after each phase of retrieving. Never rush the animal.

Once the animal has ceased to drop the dumb-bell when walking at your side, he can be taught to find the dumb-bell.

Tell the dog to "**Heel.**" Hold the dumb-bell at your right side. As you walk, drop it and proceed a few more steps. The dog will automatically sit when you stop walking. Wait a few moments before saying "**Find it.**" As you utter "find it," simultaneously gently snap the lead in the direction of the dumb-bell. When the dog approaches, he will automatically pick it up; if he doesn't, compel him to do so and instantly retreat as you gently snap the lead to you while saying "**Come.**" Upon his arrival, command "**Out**" and praise and caress him exuberantly. Also, give food. After several repetitions, the dog will respond to "find it" instantly and will love doing so if properly motivated.

The success of strict compulsion depends upon the trainer's dexterity. The whole series of actions must invariably take place at great speed, and one should not be put off by failures. If your applications are positive, the dog will learn quickly, and his submissive as well as his pack member instincts will be satisfied to a much greater degree then can ever be attained through mere obedience. Teaching a dog to do the next trick, the numbers trick, requires the strictest of compulsion. Through observation I have found that all dogs I have taught the numbers trick to have come out of it happier and more well adjusted than before this training took place. After the retrieving lesson has been learned well, the next step is to teach the animal to bring different kinds of articles. The objects used will depend upon what the dog will be required to do and the goal of the trainer. The method employed is the same throughout.

THE NUMBERS TRICK

To explain the teaching of this trick, let me first tell about its usual application in the act I do with my dog Buddy. Assume that I'm on stage with Buddy and a questioner.

"Would you please ask him an addition problem where the answer is not more than 9?" I would request of the questioner.

"Buddy, how much is 2 plus 4?" Buddy would respond by moving around a circle of tent-like figures numbered from 1 to 9; upon approaching the correct answer, he would instantly turn his head toward the number, snatch it up and continue gaiting, bringing the numbered card to me. The audience always responded with tumultuous applause. Such was the case on Johnny Carson's *Tonight Show,* Merv Griffin, Mike Douglass, David Frost, *Wonderama, What's My Line, To Tell The Truth,* Muscular Dystrophy Telethon with Jerry Lewis and stages throughout the country. Always people would ask, "How does he do it?"

"He's not really a dog," I would reply. "It's my younger brother dressed in that outfit." The guesses as to how Buddy could do math were endless and perhaps worthy of another book of a different type.

Regardless, the following pages are meant to report to you not only how Buddy does it, but also to show you how you might succeed in teaching this trick to your dog. Just about any dog can be taught it, providing the trainer is the genuine pack leader. If the trainer is not, upon completion of this trick he will be. There is no form of training more exact, punctual and binding between pack leader and pack member.

TEACHING THE NUMBERS TRICK

The dog is seated on top of a platform. As far as the animal is concerned, the platform represents his place as it did in obedience work, only now he sits in his place instead of lying down. He is taught to go to his platform through use of the same method by which he was taught going to place. The difference is that now, when he reaches the platform, he is compelled to jump up onto the platform through a snapping of the lead in that direction, and then he is made to remain seated. The primary inducement now is the word "platform" instead of "place." From anywhere within your training room, the dog must instantly respond to the word "platform" by running there, jumping up onto it and being seated. The inducements, corrections, compulsions and praise are the same as those employed with teaching "place." After three or four 15-minute sessions, the dog should comprehend the meaning of "platform" perfectly. The height of the platform should be approximately as high as the dog's shoulder is from the ground, thus enabling him to jump easily onto it.

Once the trick has been taught in its entirety, you may remove the platform if you like and have the dog perform starting from your side at a sitting position on the floor. However, for teaching purposes, the platform is necessary, as it provides an

The platform used in teaching the numbers trick should be about as high as the dog's shoulders and should be covered with a non-slip surface such as a piece of carpeting so that the dog doesn't skid when he jumps onto it.

easily visible and attainable place, or home base for the dog. He knows that after each pickup he returns to one particular spot.

The dog must be taught to remain seated on the platform until any part of your body moves toward him to the minutest degree, at which time he is to respond by leaving his platform and circling about the tent-like figures numbered 1 through 9 but not picking up any of them until hearing your auditory signal to turn toward the card and retrieve it instantly. After the pickup, he is to return to the platform and hold the number in his mouth until you tell him "**Out**."

The pickup must be as exact as a second hand on a clock, for if it takes place one second after the signal, the dog will pick up the following card in rotation and the answer selected will be incorrect. The tentlike cards should be numbered on both sides to provide easy visibility for the entire audience. The cards when standing should be about one inch below the dog's chest or parallel to his elbow so that upon hearing your signal he can quickly turn his head and in one motion grab hold of the top of the card and continue to move about without losing his stride.

After the dog has learned to remain seated on the platform, the trainer should proceed to teach him to "take it" by employing the same techniques as were employed in retrieving, only substituting the words "take it" for an almost inaudible signal made by clicking the tongue softly against the hard palate.

The trainer is to stand facing the dog. He is to hold a thin piece of cardboard in his right hand directly in front of and within reach of the dog's mouth. He is to make the clicking sound and simultaneously induce the dog to take it by pressing down with his fingers on the upper lip of the animal. The

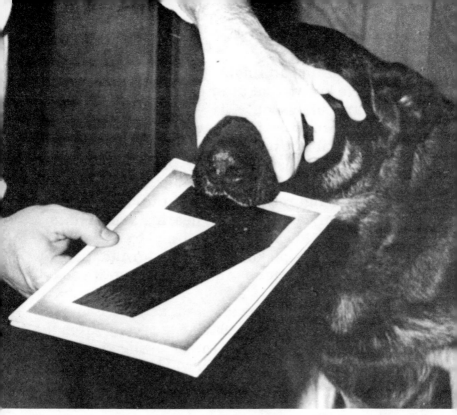

Here the dog is compelled to open his mouth so that the card can be inserted.

pressure and resulting discomfort will compel the mouth to open, at which point the right hand puts the card within the dog's mouth.

The card is to be held by the dog during several seconds of caressing and praise. If he drops the card, induce him to retake it immediately, repeating the above described procedure. After he takes the card two or three times instantly upon hearing the click and without further inducements, stop the lesson.

The following day, repeat the above procedure and now move the card to different areas, but still easily attainable for the dog. Move the card to his right and click, then move it to his left and give the click again. After each successful response offer lavish caressing and food. Allow the dog to rest for about a minute between signals. Make certain to end the lesson with the dog's having been successful three times without any inducements other than the clicking signal.

After several days of successful conditioning, fold the cardboard in half so that a tentlike structure is formed. Place this tentlike structure on the floor about three feet in front of the dog's platform.

Stand to the side of your dog while holding the lead in your right hand. The lead should be attached to the collar. Give the auditory signal. If the dog doesn't respond instantly, repeat the signal and simultaneously snap the lead downward in the direction of the card, compelling the dog to retrieve it. If when he reaches the card he doesn't pick it up, repeat the signal and simultaneously induce the pickup by using the finger-pressure technique. After he picks up, use the lead gently to induce him to return to his resting spot as you say "**Platform.**" If he drops the card before you say "**Out,**" induce him to hold it by again employing the finger-pressure method. Then say "**Out**" and of course praise and offer food. Your praise must be genuine. Continue with this procedure, placing the card to the dog's right, left, closer and farther from the platform. Each time he hears the click, he must instantly respond by moving to the card, picking it up and returning to his platform. If he hesitates, repeat the signal and simultaneously use the lead to compel him to respond. As with retrieving the dumb-bell, the dog is more submissive then ever before, and you are a stronger pack leader. End each session with pack play once again by assuming the role of a pack companion.

After one or two weeks or however long it takes,

the dog should respond immediately to the auditory signal by instantly leaving his platform, retrieving the card and returning to the platform with it. After he is perfect on lead, take it off. If he falters, return to use of the lead until he is perfect with and without one. At this point, it is time to move forward.

TEACHING THE CIRCLE

The dog must now learn to respond to your slightest body movement in his direction by leaving the platform, moving in a circle and returning to the platform.

The dog is seated on his platform. You are facing him and about three feet away. You are to hold the 6-foot lead in your right hand if the dog will circle to his left. In your left hand you are to hold a whip which you can make by using a thin stick about three feet long and attaching to the end of it a 3-foot-long thin piece of rope. The prong collar is to be turned about so as to offer less restriction. The purpose of the whip is to create the cracking sound of the whip behind the dog, inducing him to move forward. The whip need not ever strike the animal.

Tell the dog "**Circle**" and simultaneously compel him to leave the platform by gently snapping the lead. As he reaches the floor, immediately position your body by taking a step or two so that you can snap your left wrist from behind your ear and downward, creating the whiplike cracking sound one or two feet behind the rear of the dog. As you do this, hold onto the lead and simultaneously repeat "circle." The cracking sound of the whip behind the dog will induce him to move forward. Each time the dog slows down, it will be due to his not understanding exactly what you desire; this will occur quite often at first. You are instantly to repeat "circle" and

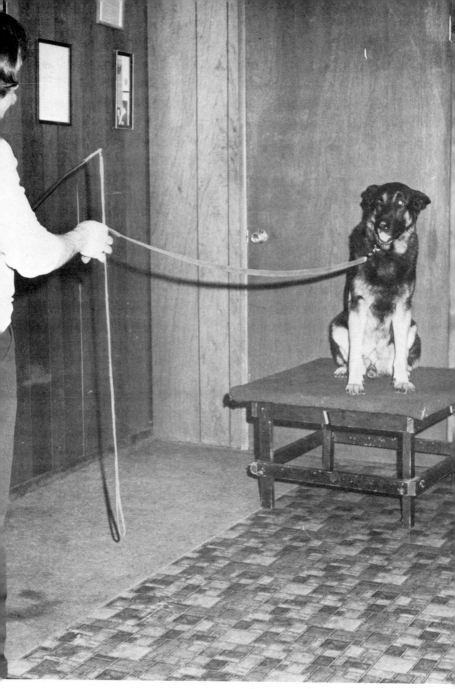

The beginning position for teaching the circle trick. Facing the dog
and holding the lead in the right hand and the whip in the other, the
trainer will force the dog to leave the platform by giving the "Circle"
command and snapping the lead towards himself.

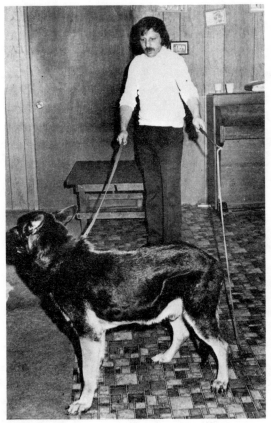

Directing the dog's circular movement is accomplished by keeping him moving by snapping the whip behind him while holding his maximum distance from you to the length of the lead.

simultaneously snap down with the whip. You will direct the animal's circular rotation while remaining within the proximity of your starting point, which will be the imaginary center of the circle. The whiplike cracking behind the dog will induce him to keep moving; because you hold onto the lead, the dog will not be able to exceed the length of the lead, thus compelling him to move in a circle. After one revolution, as the dog approaches the area of the platform, say·"**Platform**" and step toward it so that the dog may return to home base without being restricted by the lead.

After a week or two of 15-minute sessions the dog will understand clearly the meaning of "circle"; of course, as his rotating motion progresses, the snapping of the whip should decrease proportionately. It is a good idea, once the dog grasps the concept, to have him circle two times on occasion before returning to the platform. The reason for this is that after the entire trick has been learned, he may miss your first auditory signal to pick up and will have to make another revolution. To accomplish the second revolution, merely apply the whip as the dog completes his first revolution and don't slacken up on the lead, thus inducing a second revolution. At the completion of the circle trick, the dog should not return to the platform until you say "**Platform**," or indicate for him to do so by stepping toward it as he finishes his revolution.

At this point, it is time for the trainer to take another position, that being next to the dog and at his side. Since we have just taught the dog to circle to his left, we will stand at his right side. We now wish to condition him to move off in a circle when we stand at his side. This is accomplished as follows: holding the lead in your right hand, the whip in your left, say "**Circle**" and simultaneously crack the whip behind him, inducing him to leave the platform. Watch him closely. The moment that his forward movement slows even the slightest, repeat "circle" and simultaneously crack the whip behind him. If his circle is not performed so that the lead is completely extended, step toward him repeating "**Circle**" and crack the whip, thus inducing full extension. If the whip lands at the side of the dog closest to you, the aim will be accomplished.

After several days, the dog should respond to "circle" without needing inducements from the whip. At this point, take off the lead and command

"Circle." If the results are not perfect, return to the lead until the dog responds perfectly on and off the lead.

It is now time to teach the dog to leave the platform instantly and to proceed in his circular rotation at the very instant your physical being moves in his direction. To accomplish this, hold the lead in your left hand. Hold a switch in your right hand extended downward so that it is completely hidden from the dog's view by your right leg. Say "Circle" and simultaneously take one definite step with your left foot toward the dog; as you do so, from behind you tap his backside with the switch. This will induce him to move on. Repeat this several times and then decrease your movement toward the dog by taking half a step toward him as you apply the switch. He will soon, perhaps after only several days of this type of conditioning, move out at your slightest body movement toward him, for he will wish to avoid even the slightest tapping of the switch.

If he sees the switch strike him, and eventually he will, it doesn't matter, for it was hidden at your right side and from now on, he can't be sure whether it is present or not. Besides, after conditioning has taken place, he will forget the switch and respond automatically. If he doesn't, re-employ it.

A problem which may arise with some dogs is anticipation of the switch, which results in their leaving the platform too quickly. This will be corrected with the lead. If the dog moves off too quickly in anticipation, a few corrections by snapping the lead to you that compel him to remain on the platform will solve the problem.

To be most effective, the switch should be hidden from the dog's view, but you need not get fanatical about keeping it out of his line of sight.

PICKING UP THE CORRECT ANSWER

We now proceed to place nine tent-like cards, each bearing a different number from 1 through 9, printed on both faces as was earlier suggested. The dog is to respond to your slightest body gesture in his direction by leaving the platform and moving in circular formation until hearing the auditory signal, at which time he is to turn his head toward the number at his right, pick it up and continue with his circle, returning to the platform with the answer in his mouth. He is to hold the answer until you whisper "Out" and is to remain seated at his platform until you offer another body gesture for him to once again proceed with his circular rotation.

Place the lead on the prong collar with the prongs pointed inward toward the dog. Tell the dog to pick up any number you desire. Move toward him after you complete the statement. He will move out and will certainly anticipate the auditory signal and attempt to pick up the first or second card. As he attempts this, you are to instantly say "**NO**" and snap the lead in the opposite direction, preventing the pick-up. Then you are to pick up the card he tried to snatch and, holding the lead in one hand, repeat "**No**" as you slap the card against each side of his face. The light card causes no pain. This is negative reinforcement that tells the dog that he cannot pick up until he hears the signal. Repeat this procedure whenever he picks up on his own. He must respond only to signal.

Again, induce him to move forward in a circular rotation by showing body movement in his direction. If he doesn't retrieve upon auditory signal when he arrives at the desired pick-up point and continues to move on, repeat the auditory signal while he moves and simultaneously snap the lead toward you, compelling him to turn and to make the pick-up of the card immediately at his right. If he refuses to take the card in his mouth, compel him to do so by applying finger-pressure inducement and simultaneously repeating the clicking sound.

Continue to exercise the dog in this manner, but never for more than 30 minutes per session. End each session with the dog's being correct two or three times in succession. Remember, whenever the dog picks up on his own or whenever he doesn't pick up when given the auditory signal, employ the appropriate compulsions. He must turn his head and pick up instantly upon hearing the click. If he doesn't, repeat the click at another number and exactly at that moment snap the lead inward toward the number. If that problem continues to exist, you the trainer are to anticipate it; upon giving the signal the first time, simultaneously snap the lead toward the number. Only with constant practice and re-conditioning can this most complex trick be perfected.

I know of nothing more difficult to teach a dog, and I know of no trick or type of training more demanding. Successfully done, there is no type of training that will produce a stronger pack leader image for the animal, and he will be a much happier pack member. A numbers dog has a genuine place within the hierarchy of his family pack. Anyone who has ever accomplished this trick will be certain to testify to this fact.

I have taught this trick to dogs whose owners had no idea what I had done. My aim was to produce well defined meanings to the dog along with all that has been previously mentioned. The results were always most positive. The dogs were happier, more well adjusted animals understanding more clearly their position within human society.

It should also be mentioned for the sake of education and in answer to all those who have asked me throughout the years. . .

1 — No dog can add, subtract, multiply or divide. At least not within the scope or framework of human intelligence.

2 — The "ability to add" is a learned, conditioned response. The signal can be anything the trainer desires to teach, perhaps a clicking of fingernails or highly controlled electronic devices. Regardless, dog shall remain as dog and man will be man, thank God. Dogs don't eat with their elbows on the table, and man must pay taxes. Dogs don't enter into lawsuits or divorces. They are creatures relying on conditioning made possible by people when brought into man's society. If they are treated as such, they will survive and do well. They must be taught what is expected of them. How well each dog adjusts depends upon his master or pack leader's ability to read the animal and teach accordingly.

THE "PICK THE DAY" TRICK

Once your dog has learned to respond to your auditory signal of clicking the tongue or its equivalent signal of your choice, he can perform the same basic trick of moving around a circle of articles and picking up whatever you desire. For example, you can place different denominations of currency on the floor and have the dog pick up what you want him to. I recall being in a bar with several New York Mets ballplayers. I placed a one dollar bill, a five, a ten, a twenty, a fifty and a hundred dollar bill in a circle. Each of the ballplayers called out a different denomination, and of course Buddy responded by making the correct selection.

On national television shows, namely the Johnny Carson *Tonight* Show, Mike Douglas Show,

To Tell The Truth and *Wonderama*, I placed the cards representing the seven days of the week on the stage. I asked different people to call out any date they wanted. Buddy responded by selecting the correct day that particular date fell on. It was the same trick, but now instead of my supplying simple addition answers, I had to recall the entire calendar, which really is very simple. This requires about 15 minutes to memorize, because of course the first day of any month has to be one of the days of the week. For example, let's suppose that in a given year January 1 falls on a Tuesday. Therefore, January 8, 15, 22 and 29 also fall on Tuesday, because successive Tuesdays are seven days apart. If a volunteer would call out January 21 I would recall that January 22 falls on a Tuesday, therefore Jan. 21 falls on Monday. After this recollection, I would move toward Buddy, who would circle the days of the week; when he would approach the card which read Monday I would merely click my tongue and he would instantly turn toward the card, pick it up and bring it to me.

Let's suppose that the volunteer called out December 25. I would quickly remember that December 1 falls on a Friday. (That's all I have to remember. The rest is simple arithmetic.) I would quickly calculate that December 8, 15 and 22 also are Fridays, and therefore December 25 would be a Monday, an answer I could communicate to Buddy. As you see, the possibilities for creativity with regard to this trick are endless. The dog can pick up anything you desire, and it will seem as though he is doing it by employing his own faculties of reasoning, which of course is illusion. Besides, who cares? The important factor is that upon each correct completion, the dog knows of his success and the human dog pack becomes most binding and real. It is a case of dog pack member and leader communicating to the highest degree.

ANSWERING THE TELEPHONE

To teach a dog to take the phone after he has already learned to pick up an object designated by you is simply a matter of introducing a new article which he must take into his mouth or retrieve. One should start by teaching the dog to retrieve the dumb-bell. After this has been perfected, introduce the telephone and say "**Take it.**" If he refuses, induce him to take it by using the finger-pressure technique. Once the animal takes the phone immediately, merely raise it a little higher on each repetition. Eventually, he will be reaching up near to the cradle.

When a height presented is beyond the dog's reach, merely induce him to reach for the phone by snapping the lead upward with your left hand and holding the phone in your right hand. After being compelled to move upward to the phone, he will take it or be compelled to do so. After this has been accomplished, continue with the same technique, only now have the phone resting on the cradle. Use the lead to compel him to reach the cradle; if he doesn't take the phone upon command, you must again compel him to do so with the finger-pressure technique. After each completion, praise him lavishly and offer food reward. Each time you do this trick and each time you compel him to take the phone, say "**Get the phone.**"

Eventually you will be able to stand far away from the wall phone and have the dog respond when you utter your request. If he refuses, you must repeat the command "get the phone" and simultaneously snap the lead in the desired direction, compelling the animal to retrieve. The inducements and

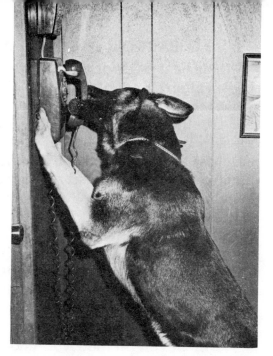

A dog's physical equipment isn't very well suited to jobs requiring the grasping of odd-shaped objects, but he can be taught to grab a telephone receiver and bring it to you upon command. Obviously, though, the dog must be big enough to be able to reach the receiver without having to jump too far upwards.

verbal commands are done in the same manner as teaching "place."

You will find that upon successful teaching of each trick, including this one, the pack relationship will become even stronger. The only physical requirement to accomplish this trick is a dog who is tall enough when standing on his hind legs to reach the telephone.

If you take your time, and don't rush the dog, this trick can be achieved generally after only a few days. The discomfort you offer the dog when employing the necessary compulsions needn't be any stronger than the discomforts required for other types of retrieving. In reality, only slight discomfort is all that is ever necessary in the teaching of any type of retrieving. If strong discomfort is required, I personally would forget the trick. A dog's physical talent as well as his mental attitude should be one that lends itself to the particular trick you desire to teach. You must try to feel and understand the individuality of your particular animal.

BARKING THE RIGHT ANSWERS

The best dogs for this trick are those that like to bark, understandably enough. You must determine what inducements inspire your dog to bark and then present these inducements for about 10 minutes per session and not more often than on three separate sessions each day. Whenever the dog responds by barking, look directly into his eyes and in a most approving voice say "**Yes.**" Simultaneously offer lavish praise and food reward. After many repetitions he will bark when you say "yes" or when you peer directly into his eyes. This is the method I use.

A stricter method is to compel barking by looking into the dog's eyes and simultaneously pulling the dog's ear. The pain or discomfort will induce barking, which you can quickly reward.

Whichever method you choose to employ, the word "yes" and the act of peering into the dog's eyes will eventually become the inducements responsible for starting him barking. You may employ other inducements. For example, each time you pull on the dog's ears, simultaneously produce the sound of the clicking tongue or fingernails. After he responds by barking, offer food to reinforce the learning. Eventually the sounds will serve as inducements. If you employ my method, the final goal will probably require more time to achieve.

After your dog responds to your eye signal or whatever you use to condition him to create instant barking, the next step is to teach him to respond when at your side. You will accomplish this in a relatively short period of time by repeating your inducements with eyes directly peering into his and in a most excited voice saying "**Yes.**" Again praise and give food. Upon perfection, it is time to teach the dog the final part necessary to perfect this trick . . . namely to stop barking *instantly* when the inducements are removed.

This will be accomplished by quickly snapping or flicking your index finger against the dog's nose as you simultaneously turn your eyes away from his and say "**No.**" He should quickly understand that barking is to stop when your eyes leave his.

This is a great fun trick for pack leader and pack member alike, but it can be accomplished only after the pack member is completely convinced that his pack position is a firm and secure one.

I have done this barking trick with my Wire-haired Terrier "Pop Corn" on the Johnny Carson *Tonight* Show, the *Mike Douglas Show* and *Wonderama*. We have also performed this trick on stages throughout the country. It provides great fun for every audience because they can visually recognize the great communication and love between pack member and leader as the dog's tail beats more quickly than his barks sound.

"SIT-UP"

Almost any dog can be taught this trick. The easiest dogs are some of the terrier breeds, Poodles, the schnauzers or any other dog that is built "boxy"—that is, one whose height at the shoulders roughly equals its length from shoulder to hindquarters. Larger breeds such as Great Danes and St. Bernards require greater physical effort on the part of the trainer and extra effort and great difficulty to the dog, and other dogs generally don't have the proper body or hind leg development necessary to support the weight of their body.

The first step would be to strengthen the dog's hindquarters as you develop his sense of balance. This is accomplished by saying "**Sit-up**" while picking up his front paws in your right hand so that his body weight is supported by his bottom. You will balance him while holding up his front paws. As you do this, praise him verbally as you caress his head with your left hand. You are to repeat this exercise every few minutes, four or five times, and keep the dog in this sit-up position for not less than five seconds or more than one minute, the exact time to be applied according to the talent the individual animal displays toward easiness of learning. Remember: don't push him.

After several days of repeating this exercise, the dog will put less weight on your palms and more on his hindquarters if you have made attempts to help him balance himself. Once he seems to rely less on your hands to support himself, it is time to employ another compulsion.

Up until now, each time you have picked up his front paws in your hand, you have said "sit-up," and as you helped him support himself you have been offering caressing and praise. When you allowed his feet to return to the floor, you offered him more praise and food. His rear musculature has developed, and so has his sense of balance and his awareness of what is expected. Now it is time to offer a new compulsion.

The dog is to be seated at your left. You are to say "Sit-up." As you command this, you are to hold your head upward so that your chin protrudes upward and outward. With the switch in your right hand, you should simultaneously flick it so that it softly strikes the dog's front paws. Naturally, he will react to this compulsion by picking up his paws. As he does so, use your lead (which is held in your left hand) to help him up the rest of the way and to balance him. If he drops his front paws, once again employ the switch. Repeat this four or five times for several days. You don't have to offer pain to the dog to get him to respond, only the slight discomfort of the switch, which is a foreign object coming into contact with his paws. However, you must apply enough compulsion to insure success. This will depend upon the talent of your dog in regard to achieving this trick and to your discretion.

After the proper amount of exercising has been done, you may now face the dog; standing 3 feet in front of him, repeat the foregoing procedure. After you have put in enough time, the dog should respond to either your auditory signal of "sit-up" or your visual signal of picking up your head. He has come to realize that each time you have said "sit-up" you have simultaneously picked up your head. At the same time, the switch has made physical contact with his paws. Therefore, the inducements will be either oral or visual. Again, I repeat, you need not strike the switch with real force against the dog's paws. Offer only slight discomfort. You are providing guidance, not punishment.

Some people feel that they can teach a dog to sit up by holding food above the dog's head. This is true, but only of those dogs whose anatomical configuration allows easy mastery of the trick. For other dogs, food alone will never work.

If the first described exercise of balancing the dog on your hand is repeated often enough, the employment and degree of compulsion required with the switch will be most negligible.

WALKING ON HIND LEGS

Again, not every dog is physically equipped to perform this trick; just as with the telephone trick, "boxy" dogs are best. Also, the dog should be at least eight months old so that his back legs are fairly well developed.

Step I: To start, the dog's hindquarters must be exercised so that his muscular development becomes strong enough to support his body weight.

This is accomplished by holding a dowel six inches long in your hands, parallel to the ground. The dog's front should rest on the dowel and be kept there with your thumbs. The pressure your thumbs apply should be only enough to prevent the dog from slipping off the dowel. No pain or discomfort is necessary.

Using a carpet as your floor to prevent slipping and thus offering the animal more security, walk with him, first pulling him toward you as you backtrack for 10 to 15 feet and then moving forward, thereby compelling him to exercise all muscles. Then send the dog back to his platform and allow him to rest for at least one minute. The entire session should not last more than 15 minutes. However, it may be repeated two or three times daily. After several days, the dog will walk more easily and with less rigidity. He will be putting less body weight on the stick as he walks to and fro. Upon completion of each compulsion to walk, offer praise and food as a reward.

Step II: After the dog seems to be moving easily on his hind legs, you should proceed to teach him to stand on his hind legs.

Hold the lead in your left hand. Hold the switch in your right hand. Say "**Stand**," which is the inducement. As you do this, the primary compulsion is snapping the lead upward. The secondary compulsion is tapping his front paws with the switch. The word "stand" should be said at the exact moment as the compulsions are applied.

If the dog has been sufficiently exercised during the first phase of this trick, accomplishing the standing phase will require only several repetitions. Be certain to offer praise and food reinforcements after each compulsion. The same results may be accomplished with only food if it is held above the

The dog's front feet are maintained on the dowel by slight pressure from the trainer's thumbs. The pressure is simply to keep the paws from slipping off the dowel; there is no need to hurt the animal.

dog, slightly beyond his reach when standing. However, the dog must be exceptionally talented for this trick if food alone is to be sufficient. Most dogs require the first method.

When the dog stands only upon the auditory signal "stand" it is time to move on to step III.

Step III: Hold the lead in your left hand and the switch in your right hand. Stand about 2 to 3 feet away from the dog and facing him. Say "**Stand.**" After he responds, say "**Come**" and induce him to do so by walking backwards and away. If he tries to lower his front feet, tap them lightly with the switch and simultaneously snap the lead up. Each compulsion should be applied gently. Again, say "**Come**" and gently snap the lead toward you as you retreat. After moving back several feet, hold the switch so that it is parallel to the ground and low enough so that when the dog reaches you he can easily use the switch to rest his front paws on. He will quickly come to realize that the distance he must walk is fairly short and that upon catching up with you, he can use the switch as a resting place. Allow him to rest on the switch for about 20 seconds; then turn about, holding the dog's paws as you do so. Then remove the switch and again retreat. When you reach the platform, allow the dog to catch up with you and once again to rest his paws on the switch for 20 seconds. Then tell him "**Platform.**" Allow him to rest on his platform for at least one minute. Five to ten repetitions for eight days will generally result in a dog who will perform this trick without use of lead or switch. After he stands and walks quite fluidly, remove the lead and in place of the switch hold a piece of food. When the dog reaches you, allow him to rest on your hands and give him the food.

Some dogs, once the lead is removed, tend to slow down in their speed of walking. In such cases, use a dowel and attach a handle to the collar (no lead). Allow the dog to rest his front paws on the dowel. As you take the dowel away and start your retreat, simultaneously snap the handle toward you as you say "**Walk.**" And of course, when he reaches you, allow him to rest on the dowel and offer excited praise and food reinforcements.

DANCING

This trick should be attempted only with those dogs who have mastered the walking trick. It requires that the dog have excellent hind leg muscular development. He will be taught to turn about and make a complete circle.

Compulsion I: Hold the lead in your left hand and the switch in your right hand. Say "**Stand.**"

From the standing posture say "**Dance**" or "**Waltz**," whichever word you prefer to be the primary inducement. As you offer the inducement, simultaneously slip the lead under his right "armpit" and quickly swing or turn him about, thus compelling him to turn. Then allow him to rest his paws on the switch.

After several seconds of resting, repeat the above procedure. Continue with this pattern until the dog turns about with little compulsion from the lead. This should be accomplished quite quickly, and no pain is necessary.

Compulsion II: Say "**Dance**" and hold the lead straight in vertical position and bunched up in your hand so that it extends approximately 3 inches above the dog's head.

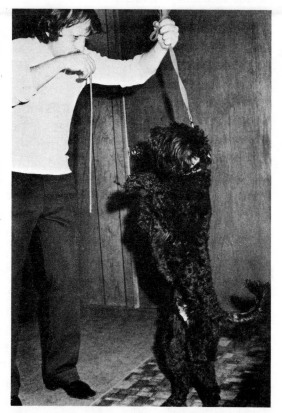

The lead held above his head will compel the dog to maintain his upright position. Remember that the conformation of the dog is important to a determination of whether he will be adaptable to being taught to walk and dance on his hind legs. Pulis and other squarely-built dogs are best for these tricks, whereas long-bodied dogs like Dachshunds are less adaptable.

As you say "dance" simultaneously move the hand which holds the lead in a complete circle, allowing absolutely no slack in the lead. This will compel the dog to turn about. Upon completion of the revolution, allow him to rest on the switch. After a few repetitions, the dog should understand what is desired.

Compulsion III: After the dog comprehends, you can increase the speed of his turns by repeating compulsion II and, as the dog turns, lightly tapping the left side of his jaws with the switch. That is, if you are teaching him to turn to the right. If you are compelling him to turn left, tap the right side gently.

Upon completion of each revolution, allow him to rest on the switch and offer excited caressing and food reinforcements.

Some dogs have a tendency to not stand straight as they turn. This should be corrected immediately by snapping the lead upward, thus compelling straight posture.

Several repetitions of sessions not longer than five to ten minutes are sufficient. If this type of training is carried out for long periods of time, the dog will become bored and upset. After the training session has been completed, enter into dog play, reducing yourself from pack leader to pack companion.

Another method of teaching the dog to turn about is with food. Just as you used the lead to cause the dog to make his revolution, you can also use food held about 3 inches above his head. This requires far more time to achieve the final goal, and the dog must have a genuine talent for dancing. Personally, I prefer the food method whenever possible. When using food, the lead must be used to help the dog to balance himself. The food is used to induce the dog to follow the revolution of your hand which holds the food, as the lead is used to help the dog to balance himself. The lead should be held up as previously described, but with this method allow a little slack. Each time the dog falters, straighten up on the lead.

Once the dog displays complete balance as he turns about following the food, the employment of the switch with light tapping against the jaw will speed up each revolution. At this point, the lead is no longer necessary. If you use this second method, be certain to work the dog before it is time for him to eat. He will be hungry and so will be more interested in chasing the food.

PLAY DEAD

Your dog should be in the sit or sit-up position. Either is fine. You should hold the lead in your left hand and a dowel about ¾ of an inch in diameter in your right hand. You should stand a foot away from your dog and facing him. Hold the lead taut.

Say "**Boom**" and exactly at that moment poke the dowel, not too hard, against the dog's left shoulder and simultaneously snap the lead down to your left, compelling the dog to lie flat on the ground.

If the dog tries to get up, compel him to remain on the ground with the lead and simultaneously repeat "**Boom**" as you re-poke softly with the dowel. Then tell him to "stay." After he understands that he is to stay, drop the lead and quickly pick up your switch. Whenever he makes the slightest move, gently tap him across the side of his shoulder or body with the switch and repeat "**Stay**." Repeat this procedure three or four times a day. After several days he should instantly respond to "boom."

The force of the compulsion to be applied in teaching and in practicing this trick in reference to both lead and dowel should be directly proportional to the requirements of the individual animal. However, pain is not necessary. Only compulsion is necessary. When you allow the dog to be free, always offer food.

MARCHING

Place the dog on his platform so that he is standing on all fours. His front feet are to be perpendicular to the shoulders and lined up with one another. Hold the lead short in your left hand.

Say "**One**" and simultaneously press down on his left paw with your index and middle fingers. The pressure exerted by your fingers will compel him to pick up the paw. Caress the paw and offer food reward. The pressure you exert must offer discomfort if the dog is to pick up his paw. Remember, this is your finger, not a foreign object such as a switch. Therefore, the compulsion must be one that offers pressure. Then, using the same hand, press down upon the other paw as you simultaneously say "**Two.**" Again, after he picks it up caress it and offer food.

Continue this exercise until you only have to say "one" as you simultaneously only point to the paw and he responds by picking it up. He must do the same with the other paw. The entire session should require no longer than 20 minutes. Naturally, this is the procedure you should employ if you want to teach only "give the paw."

Each morning and each evening repeat this exercise only five to ten times for several days. Don't make the sessions too long, as it will become boring to the dog.

After several days, the dog should respond to your one, two, three, four count as you point simultaneously with the count. The pointing as well as the rhythmic counting will be the primary and secondary inducements in that order.

The next step is to put the dog on the floor. He is to face you with his feet parallel to each other and perpendicular to his shoulders. Hold the lead and stand about 2 feet away. Say **"One"** and simultaneously with your right hand point to his left paw. He should pick it up. Then step back and say **"Come"** while his paw is in the air at its highest point. He will start to move toward you, but after he puts the paw back to the ground and starts to move in, say **"Two"** and point to his other paw. If your timing was correct, he should have taken one step in as the other paw went up. Continue moving back in this fashion until you reach the count of "four." Repeat this procedure two times a day but never more than 5 minutes in duration. After about a week, the dog should be responding perfectly. At this time, take off the lead and work the dog. If not successful, return to use of the lead.

It should be understood that not every dog has the same talent. Each is talented in different directions. I have seen dogs who could not master the marching trick, which is relatively easy, and yet could master jumping hurdles on their hind legs. We each have different abilities, and it is up to the trainer to work his dog with feeling and kindness and to evaluate the talent of his individual animal in regard to each trick attempted.

HIND LEG JUMPING

Only dogs who have excellent development in their hind legs should be taught this trick. A dog who can be taught to dance can also be taught to jump on his hind legs.

Step I: The dog should be exercised on jumping over the dowel placed at different heights for a period of a week. The dowel should be kept an inch off the floor as well as held at maximum jumping height for the dog. Generally, a total of 20 jumps per day will do much to increase coordination.

Step II: Place a hurdle which is 2 inches high in front of the dog. Hold the lead in your left hand and the dowel in your right hand. Stand to the side of the hurdle. Induce the dog to jump by saying "**Hup**." As he jumps, place the dowel in position so that it can catch his front paws before they hit the floor after the jump has been completed.

Also, as the dog's front paws hit the dowel, gently snap the lead upward, thus indicating to the animal that his front paws are not to touch the floor. After several days of only 10-minute sessions, he will respond to your signal by pushing off with his hind legs when starting his jump. This is accomplished only as a result of this exercise.

Step III: Using the same 2-inch-high hurdle, place the dog in a 4-leg standing position facing you while you stand at the opposite side of the hurdle. Hold the lead in your left hand and the switch in your right. Tell the dog "**Stand**" and with the switch and the lead compel him to do so. He must stand on his hind legs. From the standing position say "**Jump**" and simultaneously snap the lead up and over, compelling his action. Keep the switch in front of him as he lands, thus inducing him to keep his front paws from falling to the ground. If his front feet hit the ground, immediately tap them with the switch, compelling him to bring them up. Allow him to rest on the switch.

After several days of 10-minute sessions, the dog should respond to "jump" without your having to snap the lead. Continue exercising him in this

Step II in the teaching of hind leg jumping: having crossed the hurdle, the dog has its legs held up by the dowel.

Step III in teaching hind leg jumping: the switch is used to keep the dog from putting his paws down onto the floor after the jump and as a resting spot for the paws.

manner until he instantly responds to "stand" and "jump."

The compulsion of snapping the dog over the hurdle on his hind legs offers momentary discomfort and pain. I feel that most people should not attempt this type of work unless they are experienced dog handlers with extreme sensitivity in regard to offering compulsion.

FRONT LEG WORK

Only "boxy" dogs of the type described earlier are suitable for performing this trick. Generally, the trainer will encounter much difficulty in perfecting this trick because the dog's front shoulders and general body require extreme muscle development. Therefore, much exercising will be required.

Step I: The dog is placed on a platform, with his paws placed so that they are perpendicular to the shoulders and parallel to one another. The lead is held in the trainer's left hand. The trainer should be standing and facing the left side of the dog. The trainer should hold a dowel in his right hand.

The trainer says "Up" and simultaneously places the dowel against the hocks of the dog's hind legs. The trainer repeats "Up" as he uses the dowel to move the dog's hind legs upward. He moves the legs up about 3 inches and allows the legs to fall a fraction of an inch; as this occurs, he is instantly to allow the hocks to fall onto the dowel as he repeats "up." He is to continue with this procedure until the dowel is supporting the dog's hind legs in straight, upward handstand position. The trainer must use the left hand to handle the lead. The lead is used to gently induce the dog to keep his head up and body balanced with good form. The dog should be compelled to remain in this standing on front leg posture

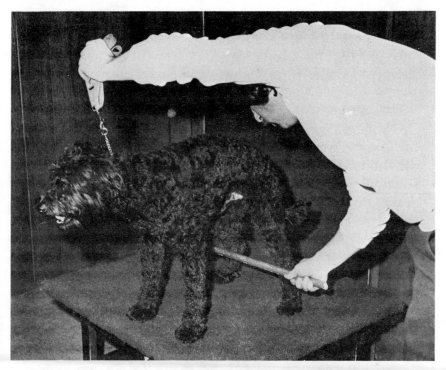

Step I in teaching front leg work: the trainer here touches the inside of the rear legs with the dowel, which will be used to support the legs as the dog's feet are forced upward.

for approximately one minute. Allow him to rest until no heavy breathing exists, and then repeat the exercise. Continue with this procedure for approximately one hour; you may work two training sessions a day. This exercise must be practiced and repeated until the dog's development is such that he is physically capable of picking up his back legs and supporting his body on his front legs for at least 5 to 6 seconds upon hearing the inducement "up." Only then do we move on to walking on the front legs. Some dogs will require one week to achieve this trick, whereas others will take longer; it depends on how much physical exercise and development is required.

When the dog begins to respond to "up" by moving his back legs upward, he will invariably at different times stop his upward movement. At such times you are to instantly induce his continuation of upward movement by use of the dowel placed inside the hocks. Once he is up, use the dowel to help him to balance himself. As the dog makes progress, take off the lead and put a handle on the collar. You will find it easier to balance the dog by employing the dowel on the legs and the handle on the collar as you simultaneously induce the dog to keep his head up.

You may use the dowel for balancing by placing it on any part of the dog's under-body which seems to help him most in balancing himself. Eventually, the progress will be such allowing you to let go of the handle and merely hold the dog's tail gently between your fingers as you employ the dowel to catch him each time he loses his balance.

When the animal seems to be fairly well balanced, allow the dowel to move 2 inches from the dog's body so that when he loses his balance you can instantly re-induce it by saying "Up" and lightly tapping the dowel inside his hocks. You will proceed to front leg walking only after the dog has been sufficiently exercised so as to be able to balance himself fairly well on his front legs.

Step II: The dog should be standing on all fours on the carpeted floor. Induce him to stand on his front legs. Employ the handle and the dowel. Once he is up, say "**Walk**" and, using the handle and dowel to help him balance himself, push the dog with the dowel, never allowing it to leave his hindquarters. Compel him to make two circles of about 15 feet in circumference and then allow him to rest on the platform.

Repeat this procedure 10 to 20 times during the hour session for as many weeks as is necessary to

Using the dowel to teach the dog to balance himself on his front legs. The animal will not be able to learn how to walk on his front legs until he is proficient at balancing himself on them.

afford the animal proper muscular coordination and development so that eventually he is able to walk without your assistance. Patience and feeling is of the essence.

The Live and Let-Live Dog

My family is composed of four children, two adults, four dogs, ten birds and an iguana, and they are all quite compatible. The dogs run together, play together and work together. They are all completely obedience-trained, thus enabling me to have complete control over their behavior at all times. They look to me for pack leadership, and one of my laws is "no fighting." On one occasion my wire-hair terrier, a male, offered challenge to Buddy for a higher pack position, but Buddy very capably physically asserted himself. He was all over the smaller terrier, and I quickly jumped in and shouted "No!" The fight instantly stopped upon my command. The laws of the pack are determined and enforced by me, the leader.

When dogs get into fights, those trying to break it up can be severely hurt. Never step between fighting dogs. Your own dog might bite you out of fury, not realizing that it is you he is biting. In the case of Buddy and my terrier, both dogs were part of my pack and were completely knowledgeable about the word "no," so they both caught themselves and stopped. If they hadn't I would have picked up the first available object, such as a throw chain or switch, and applied it only once. This would have served to break the dogs' concentration on the fight and allowed them to hear my command, re-establishing law and order.

However, the brief confrontations that come about among dogs in my household are mild in nature and very infrequent. They generally owe their impetus to jealousy: each dog wants the attention of the pack leader. Therefore, it is the job of the pack leader to work with all of his dogs. Love and attention are provided through obedience training and all other forms of training. The dog is happiest when working with and being attended to by his pack leader. It is important to provide an equal distribution of commands to all dogs and provide love to each pack member.

Recently I finished obedience training a male Doberman Pinscher that I had brought home to join our pack. He will be our fifth dog once he becomes socially orientated. When I took him home, I was certain that I had complete 100% despotic control over this highly sexually driven Doberman. I foresaw the definite possibility of his challenging Buddy and all the other males in the house. Therefore, I first made certain to prevent the fight. Buddy and each of the others went to "place" at my command as I entered our home with the Doberman on lead, completely under control in the "heel" position. Continuing with "heel," I proceeded to walk him through the house to familiarize him with his new environment. Then I attached him to a stall chain in my daughter's bedroom, which is situated one room away from where the other four dogs were lying, each in his own designated place. Next, I proceeded to test the Doberman's nature in regard to his feelings toward my other dogs. I put each of my dogs on lead and escorted them one by one into my daughter's bedroom to meet the new dog. I allowed each to become aware of the other, which they accomplished through body odors, stance, sense of smell, etc. Always, the Doberman was secured by the stall chain, and I always had the other dog in complete control with the lead. This way, if a fight were to begin, I could quickly stop it by pulling the dog on lead beyond the Doberman's reach. In each case, the Doberman offered challenge through growling and snarling at each of my males. If I had allowed the dogs to mingle right from the start without the controlled situation's having first been set up, a mad fight would have certainly ensued. However, since all concerned dogs considered me to be pack leader, I would have been able to break up the battle as previously described. But the other people in my family would have had a far more difficult time breaking up this fight, since they are pack members and therefore don't demand or get the same control as the pack leader. However, I am a firm believer in prevention whenever possible, so I introduced the dogs in the manner described so as to prevent battle. Any dog is capable of hurting another in a fraction of a second. There's simply no point to it. The only dog whom the Dobie did not offer challenge to was our Poodle, who quickly went on his back in complete submission. He offered no challenge and so pack position between the Doberman and Poodle was quickly established.

I set up a stall chain at our front door and fastened the Doberman to it. In this way he was able to observe my family pack and become more familiar with his new friends and environment. Each day for the next week, I walked each dog individually, and of course it was necessary to pass by the Doberman on the way outside. I would have the dog "heeling" at my left. The Doberman was tied to the chain so that as I passed him, he was at my right side. Thus, I stood between the dog I walked and the Doberman. And always I was ready to reprimand "no" and toss the throw chain at the Doberman upon his slightest overt act of aggression. Of course, he had been conditioned thoroughly to the throw chain before bringing him home. If he hadn't been, I would have kept him completely isolated from the others until full control had been established between him and me.

Until this point, each of my dogs was kept tied to a stall chain to prevent a fight from starting at a moment when I could not stay on top of the situation.

Once the Doberman had offered small concern as each of the other dogs passed by him on their way outside, I decided to make my point clear. The Dobie was fastened to his stall chain while my wife held the long lead, which was attached to Buddy's collar. The lead had plenty of slack, thus preventing Buddy from feeling he had the assistance of a human pack member if a fight should start. A tightly held lead suggests to the dog that the pack member holding the lead will assist him in battle, thus increasing the chances for a battle to start. Buddy at this point will not *start* a fight, but he'll fight to death if challenged. Therefore, my wife was ready to snap the lead toward herself, thus pulling Buddy out of the reach of the secured Doberman if confrontation were to be suggested. I stood about five feet to the side, slingshot ready to be used at the very instant the Doberman would offer any signs of aggression. After two corrections, the Doberman no longer growled when Buddy approached. Now, it was time to go further.

I held the Doberman on a six-foot lead while my wife held Buddy on a six-foot lead. My wife and I each held a switch. We commanded "heel" and in our living room we walked around each other in such a fashion that the dogs were close enough to touch, but each knew he was being controlled. After a minute or so, we made the dogs each lie down, thus being submissive, and facing each other. Then we stood observing waiting for each to make a move. Buddy's tail wagged against the floor. The Doberman growled in a low key. Instantly I struck the side of his face with my switch and said "**No.**" I then proceeded to spank his backside four or five times, and with each contact of the switch I said "no."

This is one law that must be established right from the start, or corrected as soon as possible. If not, the Doberman can't live with this pack. Besides, all are in danger.

After several more days of reinforcing this type of conditioning, the Doberman came to realize that whenever he offered any form of challenge, the pack leader and other pack members provided punishment stronger in nature than his need to fight. He realized it was far more pleasurable to avoid confrontation. Also, the word "no" had become indelibly clear.

Many dogs will fight with other dogs simply because they themselves recall being attacked and hurt by another dog at some previous time. In order to prevent the same thing from recurring, the dog strikes first. This is basically due to his fear of being attacked if he doesn't strike first. The more often he strikes and wins, the more confidence he gains. . . and eventually he might turn out to be the neighborhood bully.

Other dogs strike out merely from a need to be dominant or to attain high pack position. This is generally due to pride and—it is my guess, owing to many years of observation—a strong sexual drive. Such was the case with the Doberman. Therefore, in the future, I would allow all of my dogs to run free together only when I would be present to observe and preside over the situation. Eventually, the Doberman might accept Buddy to be of higher pack position. This would have to take place quite naturally, through dog language, or through physical confrontation, which I would not allow to take place.

Each time the Dobie would offer challenge, Buddy would be certain to stand up and I (the pack leader) would join Buddy in the fight. The Doberman would be certain to know his pack position within a very short time. Once he takes his proper place within the pack, he will be a happier pack member, owing to lack of frustration.

When not available to supervise, I would have to keep Buddy separated from the Dobie. When left alone in the absence of his pack leader, Buddy suffers greatly. Buddy goes from window to window awaiting my return. Such would be the case with the Dobie, my terrier and the others. It is at such times that the dog becomes more irritable, more insecure and more quick to snap and to fight with other dogs or pack members. When the leader is present, law is maintained and all are secure. . . that is, providing the laws have been established. But when the pack leader is absent, other pack members will fight, for either the reasons already mentioned or to establish temporary pack control.

My wife tells me that when I'm gone Buddy darts from window to window looking and waiting for my return and that no one can really control him. He's terribly upset; he regurgitates at times and is quick to re-assert his pack position over the others in our home. And my wife knows I'm coming home long before my arrival. Buddy starts to whine and jumps back and forth as the other pack members follow him through the house. Until the time comes that my 18-month-old Doberman accepts his pack position very definitely, even in my absence, I will be certain to separate the Dobie from the rest of the pack when I can't be around. In that way, no dog will get hurt.

Each day, the dogs of my pack will hear the doorbell ring, and together they will join Buddy in chasing to the door, barking and warning the intruder; they don't do it as individuals, but as a pack. They eat at the same time, each from his own dish. They play together under my supervision. They will be in constant contact as a pack, so quite naturally the Doberman will adjust very well.

All healthy dogs will love a puppy. Therefore, when bringing a puppy into the house, a problem rarely exists. The puppy quite naturally is accepted and loved by the older dogs, who very often adopt him as their own offspring. As the puppy grows and matures, the older dogs will maintain their superior pack positions. By the time the puppy reaches maturity, when he comes of age and feels strong enough to challenge, he will do so, unless you as the leader have established that your laws have been firmly set forth and will be enforced. Only then will the dogs work together for you. They may have little differences and quick confrontations, but nothing ever serious providing you remain as the genuine leader of the pack.

A healthy male dog will not fight with a bitch. Males will fight males and females will fight females. Both are establishing pack position. Very often the actual fight never takes place, for pack position is established through dog language, (barking, howling, gait, posture, attitude, body odors, physical strength, boldness, cunning, braveness, etc.). At times a female will bite at a male, but I have never seen it in the form of challenge. It is the bitch's way of saying "leave me alone." Then the male dog makes his own decision—that is, if the human pack leader allows him to make his decision. Regardless, he will not fight with the females; therefore, there can be no fight.

Dogs and Cats

. . . And Other Animals

Dogs who grow up with cats in the house very often become quite fond of them. Buddy, for example, loves to play with cats. Older dogs who do not like cats can be taught to tolerate them, if not to love them. If the dog is extremely aggressive, you can teach him to leave the cat alone through methods already described in regard to dog fighting and/or dog challenge for pack position; namely, use of throw cans, throw chain, the switch, and the slingshot. But remember to employ each with sensitivity and to avoid punishment whenever possible. Very often through proper introduction as I described with the Doberman, the more harsh methods will not be required. For the purpose of this book, I have intentionally described extreme cases requiring the maximum of corrective measures in the hope of enabling readers to meet all situations head-on and to solve their dogs' problems regardless of how severe the problems might be. Generally, the switch and the slingshot are necessary only in extreme cases.

Most dogs that I bring home assume their positions within the pack and adjust very happily within a few days. This is because I establish myself as pack leader and have set up the pack laws. If the dog is untrained I keep him isolated from the others; only after I complete his training do I allow introduction to take place. It is at such times that I may transfer pack leadership to one of my children. This is accomplished by teaching the child to handle and to control the animal first, to enforce the obedience commands. Then the child takes on full responsibilities in so far as caring for the animal. The child works him, feeds him, walks him, bathes him, etc. He becomes completely dependent upon the child. Of course, this can be accomplished only with the dog who is not of a stronger nature than the child is physically and mentally capable of leading. Certainly, I wouldn't attempt to put a dog like the Doberman described in the hands of my 11-year-old daughter Stacey. If he would test her powers in my absence, she might not be capable of physical enforcement.

The pack members each take turns in approaching the new dog. They sniff each other and generally the tails start to wag and play begins. When such is not the case, it is the job of the pack leader to make fighting a distasteful experience. Some breeds, such as hounds (for example, the Beagle) are more naturally inclined to chase after cats than would a German Shepherd. This is due to the inbred hunting instinct in the hound. However, any healthy dog, if properly indoctrinated to domestic life, if properly taught to understand the laws of his pack which can be established through obedience training, and providing he has a genuine human pack leader who gets whatever he asks for whenever he asks for it, can be taught to live in a home with other animals. And after living with other animals for a short period of time, generally the dog becomes fond of the others.

If from the time a puppy opens his eyes he is properly socialized, that is, he is handled by people and cared for by people and he sees cats and birds and lizards in his environment and not subjected to pain or attack from other animals, he will grow to trust and to love them. Healthy dogs strike out only to feed or protect themselves or as a reaction to a fear induced by a previous disagreeable experience. If there is no need to hunt for food and if there is nothing to fear, there is no reason to attack. Only man hunts for sport. For those dogs who have suffered disagreeable experiences, or who have been allowed to chase after cats, the described corrective methods and psychological approaches will work if applied correctly.

My oldest daughter, Elizabeth, sits at her piano playing music. Her cockatoo bird is perched on her shoulder bobbing his head in rhythm to the beat. The bird has taken a particular liking to Elizabeth from the first day he came into our home. From the first day, he sang his song to her. He is her bird. He loves every member of the family, but each to a different degree. Each of us handles him, but Elizabeth is his favorite. She happens to be blessed with a natural way of handling animals.

Stacey is seated on the couch gently stroking the head of her little black Poodle. He's her dog. She walks him, feeds him and enforces the commands as he had been previously trained to understand. He is completely dependent upon her. Therefore, she is his pack leader. He loves the others in his family, but only to the degree of each person's personal involvement with him, and their relative pack position. Stacey loves him, and is his leader. If he would be the kind of dog to offer a strong challenge for pack leadership, I would not allow Stacey to attempt to assume the role of leader. However, this Poodle is a very submissive dog who prefers being cuddled and protected. His nature is submissive enough to allow my 11-year-old Stacey to be strong enough and sensible enough to assume the role of his pack leader.

Of course, the other human members of our family pack are of higher pack position than the Poodle, so each can control him. But as was previously stated, Stacey feeds him, walks him, and takes care of him more frequently than the others in our home. Therefore, he leans on her for leadership.

Robert is rolling on the floor roughhousing with Poppy, our wirehaired terrier. Poppy is a bold, aggressive dog who at one time was almost put to sleep by his first owner. He was not socially orientated and never trained correctly; he would bite anyone he could, providing he could get away with it.

After I trained him completely, he performed on stages and also on Johnny Carson's *Tonight Show,* the *Mike Douglas Show* and *Wonderama.* He later became ill with cancer in his testicles. He was castrated. He no longer works for a living but is as scrappy as can be. He is a happy dog because he clearly understands the laws of his home. He is by nature aggressive in his play and will challenge for pack position. However, Robert is a strong, physically capable 9-year-old who can handle dogs well. He has proved to Poppy that he is of higher pack position than Poppy, accomplishing this by controlling him and getting whatever he asked for through obedience commands, first with a lead and then without one. Poppy will play rough with Robert, he will mouth Robert, he will apply pressure with his teeth, because this is Poppy's nature. But he will not bite Robert, for he knows the pack law, established by me, his pack leader.

At times Poppy becomes irritable and wants to be left alone. On such occasions he will go off to his "place," which is against the wall near the living room window. At such times, he will growl at all those who approach him, telling them to leave him alone. When he is in such a mood I am the only one he won't growl at. The children understand this, partly because they know how irritable we humans become when we don't feel well.

Steven, my youngest son, is sitting on the living room chair. Sheky, our Puli, is sitting on the floor next to Steven and is in ecstasy as the 7-year-old lovingly strokes the dog's head.

Sheky came to us at 9 months of age. His owner was a professional man, highly educated about humans. However, he had little knowledge about dogs. Sheky was not housebroken, barked too often, and was uncontrollable. One night the man, being completely annoyed, threw the Puli out of the house. The next morning the Puli was still at the front door. The man diagnosed this to be a sign of stupidity. In reality the Puli in discussion is a very dependent dog who craves pack leadership. He is a happy, sensitive animal who loves affection. He is extremely loyal and wants to be part of everything. He has no desire to be a pack leader or to leave his pack. Therefore, regardless of how poor a leader he had and regardless of how poor the pack he belonged to, he remained by the door. The man gave the Puli to the breeder from whom he had originally purchased him. The breeder, whom I believe to be a real dog lover, put the dog in my hands. We named him Sheky. He was extremely alert and very sensitive. He had been previously struck by the human hand. I know this because he would shy away from extended hands until he was certain he would be praised and not hit. If I said "no," a word he knew well, he would suddenly look so downhearted as if he had lost his best friend. When training him (teaching obedience) I took much longer to finish the job than normally is required with other breeds and dogs, owing to Sheky's extreme brightness and sensitivity. The Puli can be a great dog, but only for someone who really loves dogs. He is easily offended and when training him, I found it necessary to use food, love and body maneuverability; for example, bending over and clapping my hands when teaching "heel" to induce the dog to catch up to proper position. Also running when teaching "come," thus catering to his hunting instinct. When corrected by snapping the lead, he would seem to be let down, as if he knew that I had offered him discomfort.

I found this to be the case with Bob McAllister's Puli "Ralphie," whom I trained, as well as with the others I have worked with. A Puli should belong only to a dog lover who understands dog psychology. Bob McAllister does. His dog's radiant and apparent love for life clearly illustrates their relationship. A well trained dog who is well owned clearly demonstrates his happiness when he responds to his master's or pack leader's commands. Steven loves Sheky and Sheky loves the family. Sheky loves to work and made his T.V. debut on *Wonderama* on June 1, 1975. Everyone loved him. Buddy is pawing at the iguana, lovingly playing with him. The iguana darts across the floor and hides under the couch. Buddy pursues as his tail wags.

The other birds are flying freely, leaving their cages and returning at will. And I hear my wife saying from the kitchen, "Who's going to clean up after the birds are back in the cage?"

There is no reply.

INDEX